THE UNKNOWN GOD

A Critical History of Classical Theism

T. DOUGHERTY

SLEDGE PRESS

First edition

ISBN-10 (Paperback) 0990800865

ISBN-13 (Paperback) 978-0-9908008-6-6

ISBN-10 (ebook) 0990800873

ISBN-13 (ebook) 978-0-9908008-7-3

www.sledgepress.com

To my son,

Jacob Owen Dougherty

(Deuteronomy 32:9)

Series Preface

THE God who "rewards those who seek Him" (Hebrews 11:6) grants few gifts greater than a sincere interest in himself. Yet few in our day seem to understand the weight of this blessing; on every side, apathy abounds. Even most fellow Christians I talk to seem to want to get right to the business of practical Christian living and have little patience for abstract discussions of the nature of God or the Holy Trinity. Even within the walls of the church, theology is often met with skepticism.

This type of outlook seems to me something like a physician wanting to skip the monotonies of anatomy class to get right to the important business of surgery. No knowledge, after all, is so practical or productive as a knowledge of God. Where the gold standard of practical wisdom is to emulate God and to be holy as God is holy (see Leviticus 19:2, 1 Peter 1:15-16), must we not necessarily miss the mark to the extent that our understanding of God is unsound?

God created the world for his glory (see Isaiah 43:7, Romans 11:36, Ephesians 1:11-12, 1 Corinthians 10:31), to obtain the worship and honor due his name. Though most of our knowledge of God is derived from Holy Scripture, it is not Scripture we worship, but the God of Scripture. Yet how can our worship be appropriate if we have faulty conceptions of him? Can defective thoughts about God be anything other than unpleasant to him, even if they should appear in our prayers and praises?

To the degree that our knowledge of God is false or inadequate, so too must our worship be false and inadequate. To the extent our knowledge of God is false or inadequate, it seems we have managed to turn God himself into an idol that is something less than God. Thanks be to God who saves us not on the basis of a perfect theology—for who then could be saved?— but on the basis of our hope in his Son who died in our stead!

Space would quickly begin to fail me if I were to chronicle the ways in which a deficient knowledge of God leads to a deficiency in every other area of knowledge. God is the beginning and the end—the cause, Creator, telos, and termination point of everything. God is the meaning and context of everything. To imagine a God-less world is to take every fact out of context. Nothing can be known truly where God is forgotten.

This series intends to discuss what God is and what God is not. More specifically, it intends to address an increasingly visible disunion between ancient Christian and modern Christian conceptions of God. Ancient Christians tended to view God through a different metaphysical and philosophical lens than most contemporary Christians, and we must each decide whether to renew or abandon those ancient conceptions of God.

May our God be pleased to bless his creation again with a sincere and ardent interest in himself, and may God bless the readers of this work, whose reading itself demonstrates that they value his precious gift!

A few preliminary notes on stylistic choices may be helpful to the reader. I have chosen to use lowercase pronouns for God as many Bible translations do. I have found it to be less distracting to the eyes. I mean no disrespect to God, of course. Uppercase pronouns for God have been retained in quotations from other authors and biblical citations, as they appear in the originals. I have also chosen to use traditional singular male pronouns (as well as the colloquial "they," "them," "their," etc. used in the singular). I mean no disrespect to women either; I found this traditional usage less distracting and more in accord with biblical and Christian tradition. I have opted to use the traditional BC and AD dating, with the AD being omitted as obvious and unnecessary in most cases. Italics throughout the work are mine unless otherwise noted. Biblical citations are from the New American Standard version unless otherwise noted.

A very heartfelt thanks is due to many faithful friends who gave valuable feedback and helped with various stages of editing: Daniel Ruben, Chris Ralston, Andrew Clark, Amanda Barton, Tyler Ruff, Michelle Beauchamp, Alyssa Mako, Kelly Keener, Rachel Stadeli, Jayson MacLean, Kayla Giles, and Kristy Brown. Thanks to Rajib Datta for the illustration of Plato's cave and Wiro Tubaña for his efforts on illustrations 2-5.

So Paul stood in the midst of the Areopagus and said, "Men of Athens, I see that you are very religious in all respects. For while I was passing through and examining the objects of your worship, I also found an altar with this inscription, 'TO AN UNKNOWN GOD.' Therefore, what you worship in ignorance, this I proclaim to you. (Acts 17:22-23)

CONTENTS

1

PROFANE SYNTHESIS

THE Christian Church has historically taught that God is impassible, simple, atemporal, and immutable. Yet I suspect that the average church-goer today would struggle to describe what most—if not all—of these terms mean. Many folks, I suspect, would have never heard of any of these terms. Speaking from personal experience, I have attended a large, conservative, Protestant, non-denominational church for the past few years and have not personally heard any of these words uttered from the pulpit or stage. Whether this is a conscious choice or simply a matter of ignorance on the part of my church leaders, I cannot say with any authority. In either case, it seems clear enough that a doctrine never spoken is a doctrine that has been rejected at a practical level. Silence suggests, at least, that the subject in question is unimportant.

Before going further, it seems fitting to ask what are the cryptic, forgotten doctrines in question? Here I will offer only a cursory, preliminary definition of each, followed by a common, contemporary objection.

The *doctrine of impassibility* asserts that God does not "experience inner emotional changes of state, whether enacted freely from within or effected by his relationship to and interaction with human beings and the created order."[1] In other words, advocates of the doctrine of impassibility teach that God experiences no emotional changes. The Latin *inpassibilis* literally means incapable of passion, where "passion" refers primarily to suffering. The normative thought is that God is emotionally immovable; he never deviates in the slightest from being perfectly blessed and content. God, by such reasoning, cannot ultimately be unsettled or pained by the actions of men; nothing can disrupt God's perfect, settled repose.

In the past few decades, it has become quite commonplace for scholars to object that the Bible—from beginning to end—presents God as highly emotional. The God of Scripture seems to be full of love and full of wrath at various times and in various situations. It is not immediately apparent how the doctrine of impassibility can be reconciled with the biblical presentation of a highly emotional God. The God of Scripture, it must be admitted, certainly seems to be unsettled by human sin.

Advocates of the *doctrine of simplicity* argue that God has no internal divisions or distinctions. God is, on this account, not built up of diverse parts. God is not an aggregate of things. Rather, there is a oneness and unity within God whereby all that is in God is identical to God. Human divisions and distinctions regarding God—such as the enumeration of various, distinct divine attributes—are inapplicable to God himself, strictly considered. Each of God's attributes is said to be identical to God himself and, therefore, identical to one another. All that is in God is just God.

Yet the suggestion that all of God's predicates[2] (or attributes) are really one and the same seems quite alien to our normal, everyday way of thinking and talking about God. For example, we tend to think of God's omniscience as something quite distinct from God's

---

1 *New Catholic Encyclopedia*, quoted in Baines et al., *Confessing*, 280.

2 To "predicate," in philosophical usage, is to attribute an object to a subject. If I say, "That man over there is tall," I am predicating tallness to the man in question.

omnipresence. To *know everything* and *to be everywhere* strike us as distinctly different types of things. Yet the doctrine of simplicity requires that God's omniscience and omnipresence are really one and the same. For God to *know all* is exactly the same thing as for God to *be everywhere*. Of course, we normally don't talk about God that way. It also seems to be the case that we can't form any particularly clear conception as to how being everywhere and how knowing everything could be precisely the same thing.

The *doctrine of atemporality* is the most widely accepted of the doctrines in question. Most Christians believe that God stands outside of time. Of course, not all scholars describe God's atemporality in exactly the same way. Some scholars describe God as encompassing all time simultaneously, whereas others describe him as having no time at all.

Advocates of both views agree, however, that God does not experience time like we do. In general, the doctrine that God is atemporal places God above and beyond time. God is said to be the author and creator of time and not subject to time himself. God is said to experience no temporal succession; his reality is imagined to be static and immovable, like a motionless still frame. God is strictly timeless.

In this context, "timeless" does not mean "always relevant," in the sense that we might say a particular film or literary work is a "timeless classic." The question is not whether God is always relevant, but whether he bears a different relation to temporal process than we do. I will, therefore, use the hyphenated term "time-less" to differentiate this philosophical meaning of the term from the more popular meaning. "Atemporal" and "time-less" should be taken as synonyms in the present context, referring to God's unique, successionless state.

The question is not whether God has always existed, for everyone concerned with Christian orthodoxy agrees that he has. Rather, the question is, does God experience a sequential progression of distinct events? To ask it another way, does God have a successive, unfolding history of distinct episodes and eras like we do?

As with impassibility and simplicity, there is a growing chorus of contemporary objections to the doctrine of God's time-lessness. The practical difficulty with the doctrine is that Scripture seems to portray God as speaking and acting upon successive occasions in time. In the biblical narrative, God spoke to Adam long before he spoke to Abraham and he spoke to Abraham long before he spoke to the Apostle Paul. The God of the Bible seems to operate in time; in fact, he speaks freely about his past, present, and future in explicit terms. We even read explicitly that God's "years will never end" (Psalm 102:27) and the like.

Finally, the *doctrine of immutability* tells us that God is absolutely unchanging— unchanging, that is, in every sense of the word. God is always the same as himself, and he is always at perfect harmony with himself, existing in immovable, motionless equilibrium.

Of course, the Bible quite frequently says that God does not change (e.g., Malachi 3:6, James 1:13, Hebrews 6:18). Such passages certainly seem to require, at a minimum, that God's moral character and essential nature remain always the same. There is no danger of God becoming a liar, renouncing his promises to us, or somehow evolving into an evil supervillain. So far, all agree.

Christian scholars in the ancient and medieval world went much further than that, however, when they affirmed God's *absolute* immutability. They typically meant that God does not involve himself with change in any way at all. For example, as we will see in chapter 6, the great Augustine argued that not only does God's character not change, but neither does he change by way of participating in new activities or forming new relationships. When Augustine said that God "absolutely cannot change,"[3] he really meant it. He meant that there is no sense whatsoever in which God participates in change. God, according to Augustine, does not ever perform new actions nor does he ever form new relationships, for each of these would imply a species of change in God.

3 Augustine, *Trinity*, 5.1.3 (190).

Yet, as we will see, this created both exegetical and epistemological problems for Augustine. For example, creation in the Genesis narrative clearly suggests a change of action whereby God began to create the world after an extended period of not doing so. Genesis suggests that God began to do something which he was not previously doing and, to that extent, clearly implicates God in at least one type of change. If taken literally, Genesis suggests that God experienced something at that time which he had never experienced before, namely, the creation of our world. Moreover, God interacted with a created being for the first time, suggesting that he is not immutable in the absolute sense required by Augustine.

It seems obvious that the contemporary church has diverged quite widely from the view of Augustine. For example, few things seem more certain to the contemporary Protestant than the fact that God can carry on a personal relationship with them. Yet if God is dynamically responsive to our temporal prayers, then obviously God is reactive to external stimuli. Implicit in such a view is the assumption that God is changeable in at least one way.

These several doctrines are clearly intertwined, interconnected, and interrelated to one another; each of them serves to reinforce the others. Immutability and time-lessness, for example, are closely related concepts. If the phenomenon that we call time is strictly inapplicable to God, then it seems to make sense that God could not change in any sense. All change as we know it happens in time, after all. A timeless God would also be an immutable God, that is, a God who could not experience anything new. As far as human experience is concerned, every new experience inevitably presupposes time.

Similarly, if God is time-less and immutable, it seems to follow that he cannot have a succession of transient emotional states, for he cannot have a *succession* of anything. Succession happens in time; without time, there cannot be succession. Therefore, time-lessness and immutability each seem to demand impassibility.

Likewise, if God has no distinctions proper to himself and is "simple" in the strict philosophical sense of the word, it would follow that he could not have a diversity of emotions, because he could not have *diversity* of anything. God is always being, thinking, and acting precisely as he has always been being, thinking, and acting. Furthermore, his being, thinking, and acting are presumably all one and the same thing. Simplicity thus also seems to suppose impassibility and immutability. To a great extent, these ideas require and reinforce one another. If one of them is true, the others seem to follow. They are conceptually interconnected with one another.

Those individuals who accept the doctrines of immutability, simplicity, time-lessness, and impassibility are committed to a particular conception of God and a particular set of beliefs about him. They are committed to a particular way of thinking about Christian theology. The name commonly given to this set of systematic, self-consistent beliefs is "classical theism." In short, classical theism is the theological system which says that God is impassible, simple, time-less, and immutable.

The ancient pedigree of these doctrines is indisputable. In the early church, both the orthodox Christians as well as the Arian and Gnostic heretics accepted God's immutability and impassibility.[4] The Council of Chalcedon condemned any who refused God's impassibility.[5] The Scholastic philosophers in the medieval era all accepted each of these doctrines. Most every creed that issued forth from the Protestant Reformation explicitly affirmed each of the doctrines in question. Protestant and Roman confessions alike found a place for these doctrines, Westminster no less than Trent.

Contemporary American theologian, Richard Muller, argues that the doctrine of simplicity found broad acceptance among Christian theologians throughout the centuries:

---

4 See Mozley, *Impassibility*, 27.

5 See Mozley, *Impassibility*, 94. Not the creed proper, but some of the peripheral documents.

> The doctrine of divine simplicity is among the normative assumptions of theology from the time of the church fathers, to the age of the great medieval scholastic systems, to the era of Reformation and post-Reformation theology, and indeed, on into the succeeding era of late orthodoxy and rationalism.[6]

This assessment is undoubtedly correct and can equally be applied to impassibility, atemporality, and immutability. Conscious dissent from these doctrines has arisen only in the past 150 years or so. Several objections first arose in the United States from Old Princeton Seminary. The great Reformed theologian, Charles Hodge (1797–1878), for example, all but rejected divine simplicity.[7] His successor, Benjamin Warfield (1851–1921), explicitly rejected impassibility as a falsehood.[8]

Despite these relatively recent rumblings, historically, the Christian church taught that God is impassible, simple, time-less, and immutable. It is important to acknowledge that the term "classical theism" accurately reports the fact that the ancient, medieval, and early modern church accepted the doctrines in question with near universality. Classical theism has very deep roots in classical Greek and Latin thought.

In light of this, it seems curious that the vast majority of theologians who laud and celebrate these doctrines nevertheless concede that the Bible does not explicitly teach them. In fact, they generally recognize that a cursory reading of the Bible may leave the opposite impression in each case. For example, contemporary author, James Dolezal, is a staunch defender of the doctrine of simplicity but, nevertheless, concedes that "the doctrine of divine simplicity is not plainly revealed in Scripture."[9]

---

6 Muller, *Dogmatics*, III, 39. Quoted in Dolezal, *Without Parts*, 3.

7 Hodge, *Systematic*, 1.371-372.

8 Warfield, *Person and Work*, 570-571.

9 Dolezal, *Without Parts*, 67.

The first group of people to argue *explicitly* that ultimate reality was impassible, simple, time-less, and immutable were not Jews or early Christians, but ancient Greek philosophers. Contemporary theologian, Daniel Castelo, concludes the same and notes that "on a strictly historical view, this judgment is irrefutable."[10]

The earliest express references we find to each of these doctrines are in pagan Greek philosophy. For example, the earliest known reference to God's time-lessness is found in the writings of Parmenides in the late sixth century BC. The celebrated historian of philosophy and Anglican priest, William Inge (1860-1954), notes that Parmenides was the first to teach the doctrine,[11] and British philosopher and historian, Bertrand Russel (1872-1970), notes the same.[12]

Of course, it would be a fallacy to conclude that these doctrines are untrue simply on account of being either Greek or pagan in origin. Someone could concede the point that these doctrines originated in Greek paganism, while yet maintaining that they are compatible with the biblical and Christian conception of God. Greek thinkers, after all, asked important questions and offered answers that were, in many cases, quite profound. In cases such as that of Euclid's geometry and Aristotle's logic, we find self-conscious attempts to ground arguments not on cultural tradition or local religious authority but on propositions that seemed self-evident to all who considered them carefully. This gave Greek thought an inevitable perennial appeal. For good reason, these systems still command a great deal of respect today. The classical theist might argue that the Greeks correctly inferred God's simplicity and time-lessness from the natural world.

Among those who are more suspicious of the doctrines of classical theism, a contrary narrative has emerged in recent decades. The rebuttal might read as follows: early Christian thinkers saturated themselves

10 Castelo, *Apathetic*, 64, referencing impassibility specifically.

11 Inge, *Plotinus*, V2, 4.

12 Russel, *History*, 46.

in Greek philosophy. Early Christian theologians proceeded to read these pagan doctrines into Scripture despite the fact that they are not actually there. Such teachings are not there expressly, nor can they validly be inferred from the biblical text. As a result, ancient Christian thinkers participated in prolonged acts of eisegesis,[13] whereby pagan doctrines were *read into* the biblical narrative. This type of argument is common among those who are not convinced that the doctrines of classical theism are compatible with Scriptural teaching.

The doctrine of impassibility, especially, has not fared well in modern theological thought. Many scholars—Jürgen Moltmann being, perhaps, the loudest voice—argue that, since the God of the Bible is presented to us as highly emotional, his alleged impassibility is simply a case of ancient scholars reading Stoicism and other faulty, unbelieving philosophies into Holy Scripture.

Contemporary classical theists would do well to respond by noting that there are many Christian beliefs not explicitly stated in Scripture. The doctrine of the Trinity is a core Christian teaching by all accounts, yet the term "Trinity" cannot be found in the Bible. All Christians agree, however, that the concept of the Trinity is a valid inference from Scripture, even if not explicitly stated. The doctrine that God created the world *ex nihilo,* out of nothing, is another doctrine that is almost universally accepted by Christians but is nowhere explicitly stated in Scripture.

So we have begun to see the emergence, in crude outline, of two competing alternative systems. Both views claim to be faithful to the Bible. Both views claim to be the true, Christian view. Yet the two systems contradict one another such that both certainly cannot be true. Thus, we find the system of classical theism pitted against an unnamed alternative. To my knowledge, this unnamed alternative has not been

---

13 Where "exegesis" is "reading out of," eisegesis is "reading into" i.e., reading something into a text that is not actually there.

given a proper name, so, for lack of a more established term, I will call it *relational theism*.

The relational theist may argue against the classical theist as follows: in the Bible, God is presented as emotional, and, therefore, it is false to assert that he is impassible. Likewise, God is presented as operative in time, so there is no basis upon which to assert that God is time-less. Likewise, the Bible presents God as having diverse attributes such as omnipotence and omnipresence, and we find no hint that these diverse attributes are really all one and the same. Relational theists generally teach that although God's nature and essential attributes do not change, God most certainly participates in new activities such as creation and the active redemption of man. God also certainly enters into active, responsive, temporal fellowship with each Christian.

We might well distinguish between God's *absolute immutability*, as taught by the classical theist, and what we might call God's *essential sameness*, as taught by the relational theist. All Christians who accept the authority of Scripture will agree that God's character does not change. A God with a whimsical character could not be perpetually trustworthy, which would be disastrous to our faith and trust in him. So far, all agree. Classical theists, such as Augustine, typically add to this that God does not form any new external relationships or participate in any new activities either. These additional points are the real grounds of contention. It is one thing to say that God's nature and character do not change; it is something else entirely to say that God does not perform new actions or respond to external stimuli. Relational theists insist that God is dynamically responsive to the temporal thoughts and actions of every individual; he carries on a personal relationship with every creature he has made.

Relational theists are generally quick to point out that the burden of proof for each of these doctrines seems to rest on the shoulders of the classical theist. For if one man says that "God is simple" and another man denies the same, the burden of proof rests naturally on the one making the positive claim. In a Protestant context, the classical theist will be required to demonstrate that Scripture necessitates the inference in question.

It is also worthy of note that classical theists tend to be strong realists, whereas relational theists tend much more often to be nominalists or conceptualists. For example, classical theists traditionally argue that God is identical to his own goodness. The doctrine of simplicity seems to require that since God is good, God must be goodness, as such. Goodness, on this account, is a particular, personal, concrete[14] being, namely, God.

Relational theists typically argue that this is a confusion of categories. To the relational theist, "goodness" is much more likely to be described in purely nominal or conceptual terms. Goodness is neither a physical entity nor a spiritual entity; rather, it is only a concept and concepts exist only within the mind. "Goodness" is, on this account, merely a conceptual assessment or evaluation. Beings cannot literally *be goodness* because "goodness" is merely a generic, evaluational term. Beings cannot literally *be goodness* any more than they could literally *be badness*. These terms are purely evaluational, pointing to our relative approval or disapproval. The relational theist generally insists that "goodness" is purely adjectival or adverbial, whereas the classical theist insists that Goodness is, ultimately, a proper noun, identical to the being of God himself.

As the title suggests, this book is a history of classical theism. In other words, it is a history of the doctrines of impassibility, simplicity, time-lessness, and immutability. We will survey the writings of a

---

14 By "concrete" I mean simply an existent object, i.e., a thing or person that actually exists. Such objects can be physical or spiritual. God is a concrete being. I am a concrete being. The chair I am sitting on is a concrete object. Concrete is typically contrasted with abstract, where something "abstract" exists only as a concept in the mind. Fictional characters, for example, are not concrete beings, but rather abstract concepts.

number of Christian thinkers throughout the centuries, in chronological order. We will also consider a few non-Christian thinkers who nevertheless affirmed those several doctrines associated with classical theism. These sketches are not intended to be general accounts as one might find in a history of philosophy. My specific interest is with the doctrines outlined above. What made these doctrines attractive and compelling? What arguments were given in their defense? What conclusions did they yield about the human knowledge of God?

This survey is far from comprehensive. I will cover only the most important thinkers and the most relevant currents of thought. A host of intermediate figures will be mentioned only in passing, if not simply passed over in silence. I will limit the inquiry to a select few topics in the realms of theology, epistemology, and metaphysics.

I have allocated more space to Plato and Plotinus whose pagan philosophical systems are likely to be less familiar to the contemporary Christian reader. Even in these chapters, however, I will not give attention to subjects such as the development of formal logic, natural science, ethics, or political science, as these topics are outside of my present scope and concern. Furthermore, I have not given much emphasis to the biographical details or historical context of the various thinkers; thought will here be judged simply as thought.

I have tried to avoid authors who are widely regarded as heretical, as my interest is in mainstream, orthodox Christian tradition. Copious citations from each thinker will help to defend each point; the reader need not take my word for anything that they can see with their own eyes. As a result, the chapters are dense with extended quotations. The reader will have to forgive me for whatever aesthetic deficiencies result from this approach. It seemed necessary on account of the polemic nature of the work.

The absence of a chapter on Aristotle may seem a grave and conspicuous defect in the selection of thinkers, but, as will become clear through the course of the work, Aristotle was, to a large extent, in agreement with Plato on subjects such as the simplicity, immutability, and impassibility of ultimate reality. Aquinas, who preferred Aristotle, found little reason to differ with Augustine, who preferred Plato, because Plato and Aristotle agreed that God was simple and strictly unchangeable. Indeed, the relative agreement of Plato and Aristotle did much to enforce these doctrines in early Christian philosophical consciousness.

The notion of the unbiased historian has long been discredited as mythological, so I will make no pretense of neutral disinterest. The selection of thinkers itself is undoubtedly a form of bias, and I suspect the reader will not make it very far into the narrative before perceiving which side of the debate the author lands on. Given such a circumstance, I can do no better than to reveal my particular bias so that the reader knows what sort of simpleton or scoundrel they are dealing with. My frank admission, then, is that I am a relational theist in the sense that I have outlined above. Necessary qualifications aside, I do not believe that the Bible teaches that God is simple, time-less, immutable, or impassible, nor do I think that these doctrines can be validly inferred from Scripture, nor do I think that they are compatible with Scriptural teaching.

I could be wrong, of course. I claim no infallibility. I am a simpleton at heart, and, as a simpleton, perhaps I have oversimplified. Perhaps I've been foolhardy in thinking I could somehow fit God into this meager brain of mine. Perhaps Christian theology is not meant to be reasonable to finite man, and the great mistake I made was that I tried to force inherently non-reasonable truths to fit neatly into the tidy scheme of human rationality. In my defense, however, if it be conceded that some of our Christian doctrines are not ultimately rational, it would seem to follow that such doctrines are incapable of giving a rational defense of themselves. Such a view would certainly have its own set of serious problems. It seems to me that rationality always inevitably maintains an inherent competitive advantage.

In any event, it cannot be denied that countless brilliant and godly men have defended the doctrines in question vigorously and wholeheartedly. A great many men were willing to die upon this hill, and, perceiving the weight of this fact, I have made every effort to give careful and honest presentations to each thinker. The Christian Church should, of course, come to a consensus on these doctrines and I am conscious of the fact that straw men—however fun to set up and knock down—won't get us very far unto that end.

The present work aims to be a history, and it also aims to be a *critical* history. I will freely comment upon tensions, internal inconsistencies, difficulties, etc. I will freely offer common counter-arguments and rebuttals.

The classical theist will find encouragement in the fact that the historic Christian church indeed taught classical theism. Undoubtedly, we will see a high degree of uniformity and agreement among the various thinkers. Honesty requires the admission, however inconvenient. Part of my motivation in undertaking this work was to give an account of those factors that led to the widespread acceptance of these doctrines among early Christians. This seemed to me the first step in refuting classical theism, which I hope to take a further step towards in the second volume of the series.

The reader will understand, then, that I accept as true that narrative which says that these are false, pagan ideas that were read into Scripture throughout the centuries. I have been heavily influenced by scholars such as Hodge, Warfield, Nicholas Wolterstorff, and Alvin Platinga. These men each raised serious and sustained objections to one or more of the doctrines of classical theism. They argued that the doctrines of classical theism are of suspicious lineage and contradict other Christian doctrines which are much more clearly taught by Scripture.

Our history of classical theism will undoubtedly reveal a high degree of uniformity among the various thinkers, but I believe it will also consistently reveal a serious pitfall. Classical theists always arrived at the striking conclusion that God, in the final analysis, cannot *properly* be known by man. Though man may know God by way of human metaphors and analogies, such metaphors cannot describe God as he really is. This apparent skepticism about God's knowability seemed a simple inference from the doctrines of time-lessness, immutability, and simplicity. For humans are neither time-less, nor immutable, nor simple. I can think neither time-lessly, nor simply, nor immutably. If God is simple, immutable, and time-less, and I certainly cannot think about God in those terms, then I cannot know God as he really is. I will argue that this epistemological skepticism is an unfortunate inheritance from paganism.

Where to begin? When Alexander the Great conquered the known world in the fourth century BC, Greek thought and language conquered the world with him. Our New Testament, written primarily by Hebrews, yet in Greek, serves as a recurring reminder of Alexander's success. Within the sphere of Christian philosophical theology, the classical Greek philosopher Plato (c. 428–c. 348 BC) would become the decisive voice. As we will see in the next chapter, Plato taught that ultimate reality is impassible, simple, time-less, and immutable. Yet this created serious epistemological problems for Plato, because this type of reality seemed far removed from our own. The "Demiurge" of Platonism is more akin to a disconnected and unknowable "divine watchmaker" of deism than the immanent and caring God of Holy Scripture.

It is no mere coincidence that after Plato's death, his school in Athens turned to formal skepticism, especially after the third century BC. Skepticism in theological matters seemed the inevitable result of the Platonic conception of God. The statue to the "UNKNOWN GOD" that the Apostle Paul stumbled upon in Athens (see Acts 17:23) was almost certainly inspired by Platonism in part. Plato and his successors, as we will see, made God unknown and unknowable.

The unparalleled success of the Platonic philosophy in the ancient world led, in countless instances, to Christian attempts to discover

Platonic philosophy in Scripture, particularly in the doctrine of God. In my view, classical theism is Christianity interpreted through the lens of Platonic and Neoplatonic philosophy. The attempted harmonization of Plato's god with the God of the Bible began very early. Justin Martyr (100-165 A.D), for example, was comfortable referring to the Christian God as the Demiurge.[15] It was a common sentiment among early Christian thinkers that Plato's god and the God of the Bible were practically one and the same. In chapter 4, we will see that this teaching was explicit in Clement of Alexandria. In chapter 6, we will find it even more explicitly in Augustine.

Attempts to synthesize Platonism with Christianity were strenuous and recurrent until the Protestant Reformation in the 16th century. Powerful intellectual forces gave impetus to this work. There was, for example, a strong intellectual bias in both antiquity and the medieval period which sought to reconcile conflicting points of view to the farthest extent possible. William Inge is undoubtedly correct in saying:

> This deference to antiquity [was] always prominent in classical literature... Thinkers under the empire felt it to be incumbent on them to harmonise differences as far as possible, as though the divergent views of the ancients were but superficial discrepancies covering a fundamental unity.[16]

Rather than advocating for strong lines of demarcation between Christian and pagan beliefs, ancient Christian scholars often sought to harmonize and synthesize a variety of viewpoints. A high degree of deference to well-respected earthly authorities led to the synthesis of contrary and sometimes even contradictory ideas.

It is commonly recognized that modern man is much more individualistic than his ancient counterpart. Where modern man places a

---

15 See Copleston, *History*, V2, 17.

16 Inge, *Plotinus*, V1, 110.

high premium on uniqueness, originality, and novelty, each of these was viewed as a crime by ancient man. Modern man views himself as a unique individual, distinct from the group, whereas our ancestors viewed themselves as indivisible from the group. Though quite counterintuitive to us, the word "individual" actually meant "indivisible" until about 1750 when it acquired its modern implication of separateness and isolation. This dramatic inversion in the way that man viewed himself in relation to his fellow man would—with seeming inevitably—fan the flames of the French and American revolutions later in the same century.

Ancient man's mentality was, to a much greater extent, a collective, group mentality.[17] Serious disagreements were often covered over by allegorical (or otherwise superficial) modes of interpretation. Every author was seemingly given the benefit of the doubt that he agreed with the group, even if his actual words suggested otherwise. We shall call this the ancient and medieval *synthesis bias*. Plato, in particular, was almost universally regarded as a well-respected, honest thinker who got a great many things correct about God. We will discover a number of instances where Christian theologians suggested that Plato was a true Christian believer. A number of early Christian scholars even raised the suggestion that Plato was an inspired prophet of the one, true God.

Not unlike my own thesis, the esteemed American church historian, Jaroslav Pelikan (1923-2006), suggested that Christian orthodoxy still retains foreign elements:

> It is true that in its language and sometimes in its ideas orthodox Christian doctrine still bears the marks of its struggle to understand and overcome pagan thought, so that what

17 It was in no small measure the influence of Christianity through the centuries that led to the modern conviction that each man is a unique individual, accountable to God for himself alone. This seems one of the unspoken *solas* of the Reformation.

> later generations of the church (including those generations that were themselves ignorant of antiquity) inherited in the dogma of the church included more than a little of Greek philosophy as well. Victory over classical thought there assuredly was, but a victory for which some Christian theologians were willing to pay a rather high price.[18]

Pelikan noted that a person need not have direct contact with the original pagan sources to be influenced by them through secondary sources. A child who learns orthodox teachings in Sunday school hasn't yet read very much of the Bible and certainly hasn't yet read very many of the dialogues of Plato. The young convert simply hasn't the means to judge whether or not the orthodoxy they were taught also included a tinge of pagan philosophy.[19]

Even more to the point, William Inge argued that "Neoplatonism is part of the vital structure of Christian theology, and it would be impossible to tear them apart."[20] Inge is correct, in my judgment, that Christian theology is inundated with elements of Platonism and Neoplatonism. Inge had great sympathies with Platonism and took the synthesis of Christianity with Platonism to be a happy and fortuitous turn of events. Inge was a classical theist in the sense I have defined it. Of course, I don't quite see it that way.

In my view, Christian educators—in seminaries and Sunday schools alike—still teach a watered-down form of Neoplatonism in which God is made so transcendent that he becomes unknowable, both personally and intellectually. The God of the Bible is turned into the Platonic idol to the UNKNOWN GOD.

Greek philosophers were relatively consistent with these doctrines and brought them to their logical conclusions. However, from the start,

---

18 Pelikan, *Christian Tradition*, 45.

19 I borrowed the thought, no doubt, from Thomas Kuhn.

20 Inge, *Plotinus*, V1, xiii.

they fit awkwardly into the Christian framework. Men like Augustine (chapter 6) and Aquinas (chapter 8) were forced to make so many exceptions to these doctrines that they emptied them of their original significance and meaning. To the extent that early Christians were consistent with these doctrines, they turned either toward an irrational mysticism or, in cases like that of Dionysius the Areopagite (chapter 7), to a covert pantheism.

By accepting many of Plato's teachings about ultimate reality, early Christian thinkers inherited the same conceptual problems that plagued the Platonists, and they arrived at nearly identical conclusions. The end result was always the same: a deep and residing pessimism about the knowability of God. We will see the theme recur, like a bad case of déjà vu, in every single thinker in this volume.

Undoubtedly, the Protestant Reformation had a purifying influence as it purged ancient errors and biases from Christian theology. The Reformers insisted that the authority of Scripture is unique and solitary. The method of ancient synthesis was, in large part, rejected. Philosophical speculation was made subordinate to sound Scriptural exegesis.

In principle, this should have purged Christianity of those Platonic elements that had crept in over the centuries. However, the scope of the Reformation was far from comprehensive. The focus of the Reformation was not the doctrine of God (theology proper) but rather the question of ultimate authority (ecclesiology) and the manner of human salvation (soteriology). That focus had laser precision and an astonishing degree of accuracy and insight, but the work remains incomplete. The medieval and Scholastic doctrine of God, filled with Platonic and Neoplatonic error, was accepted with little emendation. In my view, a profane synthesis still prevails.

2

Plato's Theory of Ideas

THOUGH the doctrines of impassibility, simplicity, time-lessness, and immutability are found in the extant writings of a number of Greek philosophers who lived earlier than Plato, it was primarily through the influence of Plato that these doctrines received broad acceptance in Christian tradition. Our survey begins, therefore, with Plato (c. 428–c. 348 BC).

In hopes of better understanding why early Christian thinkers sympathized with and even adopted some of Plato's ideas, we must first survey the general character and tenor of Plato's thought. I do not want to assume that every reader is already familiar with the works of Plato. My agenda in this chapter is, therefore, very limited; we will review the general tendencies and patterns of Plato's thought, especially his theory of Forms (or Ideas). To state my intentions plainly, I think we have to understand something of Plato in order to understand the ways in which Platonic ideas were later assimilated into Christian orthodoxy.

Plato was born about the time the Old Testament was completed.[1] He was born into a well-to-do family in Athens, in an age not

1 By most accounts, the Old Testament was completed around 420 BC.

entirely unlike our own: men had grown skeptical of the idea of absolute truth. The elder Protagoras (481–411 BC) had argued that man—each man—is the measure of truth unto himself. According to Aristotle, Protagoras "said that man is the measure of all things, meaning simply that that which seems to each man also assuredly *is*."[2] One could speak of personal, private truths, but an objective truth for all men was deemed an impossibility. One man's truth cannot be imposed upon another.

Though relativism (to use a much later term) had become common in Greek society, Plato saw it as self-defeating. He was quick to point out that there is a measure of hypocrisy involved in an educator collecting a fee to teach that all opinions are equally legitimate. In one of Plato's dialogues, Socrates is made to object:

> And now, I said, I will ask my stupid question: If there is no such thing as error in deed, word, or thought, then what, in the name of goodness, do you come hither to teach?[3]

According to Plato, Protagoras' relativism precluded the possibility of education, because education, in its very conception, supposes that some opinions are more legitimate than others:

> For if...no man...has any superior right to determine whether his opinion is true or false, but each, as we have several times repeated, is to himself the sole judge, and everything that he judges is true and right, why, my friend, should Protagoras be preferred to the place of wisdom and instruction, and deserve to be well paid, and we poor ignoramuses have to go to him, if each one is the measure of his own wisdom? … I say nothing of the ridiculous predicament in which my own midwifery and the whole art of dialectic [i.e., philosophical

2 Aristotle, *Metaphysics*, 1062^{b}[10], 590.

3 Plato, *Euthydemus*, [287], 73.

> debate] is placed; for the attempts to supervise or refute the notions or opinions of others would be a tedious and enormous piece of folly, if to each man his own are right.[4]

In addition to excluding the possibility of education, Protagoras' relativism seemingly ruled out the possibility of ignorance, false opinion,[5]expertise,[6] wisdom, and folly.[7] If Protagoras was consistent, according to Plato, he would conclude that the opinions of wise men are no more legitimate than those of a tadpole or a "dog-faced baboon."[8] According to Plato, "there are many ways...in which the doctrine that every opinion of every man is true may be refuted."[9]

Christian authors have always found great affinity with Plato's stance against the sophistic relativism of his day, and rightly so. Such a stance is sorely needed in our day. Plato noted that relativism faces a coherence problem because it asserts that relativism applies to all men at all times. Relativism thus always presents itself as universal and absolute, thereby defeating itself.

Plato argued that relativism undermined ethical behavior. He attributed much of the cultural decay in Athens to a faltering sense of truth and falsehood. When a sense of absolute truth is lost, so too is the sense of absolute right and wrong. Plato argued that a belief in objective truth is indispensable for human knowledge and ethics alike. He said that ethical virtues "are not relative to individuals" and "must be supposed to have their own proper and permanent essence: they are

---

4 Plato, *Theaetetus*, [161-162], 522.

5 see Plato, *Theaetetus*, [170], 527.

6 see Plato, *Theaetetus*, [178], 531.

7 see Plato, *Cratylus*, [386], 86.

8 Plato, *Theaetetus*, [161], 522. In his autobiography, Darwin expressed a similar concern. If man evolved from beasts, and is, as such, just another beast, why should man's opinions be valued more highly than that of the other beasts?

9 Plato, Theaetetus, [179], 532.

not in relation to us, or influenced by us, fluctuating according to our fancy, but they are independent, and maintain to their own essence the relation prescribed by nature."[10]

Likewise, a true proposition is always true: "A principle which has any soundness should stand firm not only just now, but always."[11] A true proposition is true at all times, regardless of the shifting sands of popular opinion:

> For not to know the nature of justice and injustice, and good and evil, and not to be able to distinguish the dream from the reality, cannot in truth be otherwise than disgraceful to him, even though he have the applause of the whole world.[12]

Plato recognized, however, that the physical world we live in seems far removed from the unchanging truths thus described. The physical world is neither time-less nor unchanging. A man who is handsome at twenty years old is less so at age sixty, and is a worm-eaten monstrosity at the age of 150. When we talk of "whether a face is fair, or anything of that sort...all such things appear to be in a flux."[13] The physical world changes. Popular opinion changes. Language changes. Our bodies change. Our senses dull with age. In the physical world, nothing whatsoever escapes the all-pervasive flow of time and change. Greek philosophers referred to this situation of continual discontinuity and uncertain fluctuation as "the flux." How can we hope to find timeless, unchanging truths in such a predicament? The possibility of true knowledge seemed doubtful at this stage:

> Nor can we reasonably say that there is knowledge at all, if everything is in a state of transition and there is nothing

10 Plato, *Cratylus*, [386], 86.

11 Plato, *Meno*, [89], 184.

12 Plato, *Phaedrus*, [277], 140.

13 Plato, *Cratylus*, [439], 113.

> abiding; for knowledge too cannot continue to be knowledge unless continuing always to abide and exist. But if the very nature of knowledge changes, at the time when the change occurs there will be no knowledge; and if the transition is always going on, there will always be no knowledge, and, according to this view, there will be no one to know and nothing to be known: but if that which knows and that which is known exist ever, and the beautiful and the good and every other thing also exist, then I do not think that they can resemble a process or flux, as we were just now supposing. Whether there is this eternal nature in things...is a question hard to determine.[14]

This dilemma is central to Plato's thought. If the changing world is all that exists, then all we could posit are relative truths and relative virtues. If all of reality is in perpetual flux, Protagoras surely had the better of the argument. What one society describes as justice may seem unjust to another society. What seems true today, from one point of view, may be deemed false in a hundred years time from some other point of view. If the changing world is all that exists, this conclusion seems to be inevitable and inescapable.

Moreover, according to Plato, the physical sensations by which we obtain much of our knowledge are themselves changing and, therefore, unreliable. A large object appears very small when seen from a great distance, but this is an illusion. The oar of a boat appears straight out of water, but crooked when seen in water.[15] We often misjudge our footing and stumble. We are prone to the deceptions of illusionists and magicians. Our faculties grow increasingly unreliable as we progress past the prime of life. Yet if there is true knowledge—fixed philosophical knowledge—then it must have an abiding permanence which

14 Plato, *Cratylus*, [440], 113.

15 Plato, *Republic*, [602], 431.

transcends the changing world of sense perception. For example, if the truths of mathematics are always true, they must seemingly appeal to some higher authority than a changing, material world. The solution proposed by Plato would become—and almost certainly will remain—the most famous philosophical theory in history, the so-called Theory of Ideas (or Theory of Forms).

Plato argued that there must be an unchanging, intangible realm beyond the world of change and of sense perception. Though individual instances of beauty, for example, are relative and quickly fading in this physical realm, true beauty—beauty in its essence—must remain permanently fixed and static in that other realm. Plato discussed the character of these unchanging essences in a lengthy dialogue between Socrates and Cebes of Thebes (c. 430–350 BC). He is here worth quoting at length. Socrates begins:

> Is that idea or essence…of equality, beauty, or anything else—are these essences, I say, liable at times to some degree of change? Or are they each of them always what they are, having the same *simple* self-existent and *unchanging* forms, not admitting of variation at all or in any way, or at any time?
>
> They must always be the same, Socrates, replied Cebes.
>
> And what would you say of the many beautiful—whether men or horses or garments or any other things which are named by the same names and may be called equal or beautiful,—are they all unchanging and the same always, or quite the reverse? May they not rather be described as almost always changing and hardly ever the same, either with themselves or with one another?
>
> The latter, replied Cebes; they are always in a state of change.

And these you can touch and see and perceive with the sense, but the unchanging things you can only perceive with the mind—they are invisible and are not seen?

That is very true, he said.

Well then, added Socrates, let us suppose that there are two sorts of existences—one seen, the other unseen.

Let us suppose them.

The seen is the changing, and the unseen is the unchanging?

That may be also supposed.

And, further, is not one part of us body, another part soul?

To be sure.

And to which class is the body more alike and akin?

Clearly to the seen—no one can doubt that.

And is the soul seen or not seen?

Not seen.

Unseen then?

Yes.

Then the soul is more like to the unseen, and the body to the seen?

That follows necessarily, Socrates.

And were we not saying long ago that the soul when using the body as an instrument of perception… that the soul too is then dragged by the body into the region of the changeable, and wanders and is confused; the world spins round her, and she is like a drunkard, when she touches change?

Very true.

> But when returning into herself she reflects, then she passes into the other world, the region of purity, and eternity, and immortality, and unchangeableness, which are her kindred, and with them she ever lives, when she is by herself and is not let or hindered; then she ceases from her erring ways, and being in communion with the unchanging is unchanging. And that state of the soul is called wisdom?
>
> That is well and truly said, Socrates, he replied.[16]

Beautiful things in the physical world are perpetually changing. Yet, according to Plato, true beauty has an enduring and unchangeable life in the soul of man. Our visible body is subject to change, but our invisible soul somehow communes with unchanging ideas. Although most men do not care to look further than physical beauty, the philosopher reflects on beauty itself, beauty in its essence. He enters into "the other world" and has "communion with the unchanging." In communing with the unchanging, he himself acquires an unchangeable knowledge. He leaves behind the world of sense and enters a world of static repose. For Plato, the constant changes and alluring enticements of the physical world often distract us from the more important work of contemplating unchanging truth.

Plato thus described reality as existing in two distinct layers or modes. There is, on the one hand, the well-known physical world, which is in a state of perpetual change or flux. Yet, on the other hand, Plato also believed that there is a lesser-known reality which is altogether static and unchanging. Here beauty changes, but there beauty is always at one with itself, identical to itself.

The philosopher overcomes the limitations and deficits of the changing body as he enters this eternal and unchanging realm through "the mind's eye."[17] Things that are beautiful in this physical realm are

---

16 Plato, *Phaedo*, [78-79], 231-232.

17 see Plato, *Republic*, [518], 389.

identified as such only because they "partake" or have a "participation" in absolute beauty in the unchanging realm. A thing "can be beautiful only in so far as it partakes of absolute beauty."[18] What a shadow or a reflection in a pond is to the object casting the shadow or reflection, so too is this present world of physical sensation likened to that realm of simple and time-less absolutes.[19] This world is hazy, changing, uncertain, where that world is clear, static, and enduring. This world is subject to the whims and fancies of time and flux, but that world is time-less. This world is *becoming*, but that world is pure, unchanging *being*.[20] By successive steps, reason learns to move away from the world of sensation and to uncover the world of unchanging ideas within the intellectual realm of the soul. The philosopher focuses on the unchanging laws of mathematics and weighs the unchanging principles of truth, beauty, and justice.[21]

Plato embodied and immortalized this central theme with a memorable allegory of an underground cave or den. I feel again compelled to quote him at length:

> And now, I said, let me show in a figure how far our nature is enlightened or unenlightened:—Behold! Human beings living in an underground den, which has a mouth open towards the light and reaching all along the den; here they have been from their childhood, and have their legs and necks chained so that they cannot move, and can only see before them, being prevented by the chains from turning round their heads. Above and behind them a fire is blazing at a distance, and between the fire and the prisoners there is a raised way; and you will see, if you look, a low wall built

18 Plato, *Phaedo*, [100], 242.

19 Plato, *Republic*, [510], 387.

20 see Plato, *Timaeus*, [28], 447.

21 Plato, *Republic*, [509], 386.

along the way, like the screen which marionette players have in front of them, over which they show the puppets.

I see.

And do you see, I said, men passing along the wall carrying all sorts of vessels, and statues and figures of animals made of wood and stone and various materials, which appear over the wall? Some of them are talking, others silent.

You have shown me a strange image, and they are strange prisoners.

Like ourselves, I replied; and they see only their own shadows, or the shadows of one another, which the fire throws on the opposite wall of the cave?

True, he said; how could they see anything but the shadows if they were never allowed to move their heads?

And of the objects which are being carried in like manner they would only see the shadows?

Yes, he said.

And if they were able to converse with one another, would they not suppose that they were naming what was actually before them?

Very true.

And suppose further that the prison had an echo which came from the other side, would they not be sure to fancy when one of the passers-by spoke that the voice which they heard came from the passing shadow?

No question, he replied.

> To them, I said, the truth would be literally nothing but the shadows of the images.[22]

Plato here envisioned men who are chained in such a way that all they ever see are shadows on a wall (or screen) in front of them. Plato's cave can be illustrated as follows:

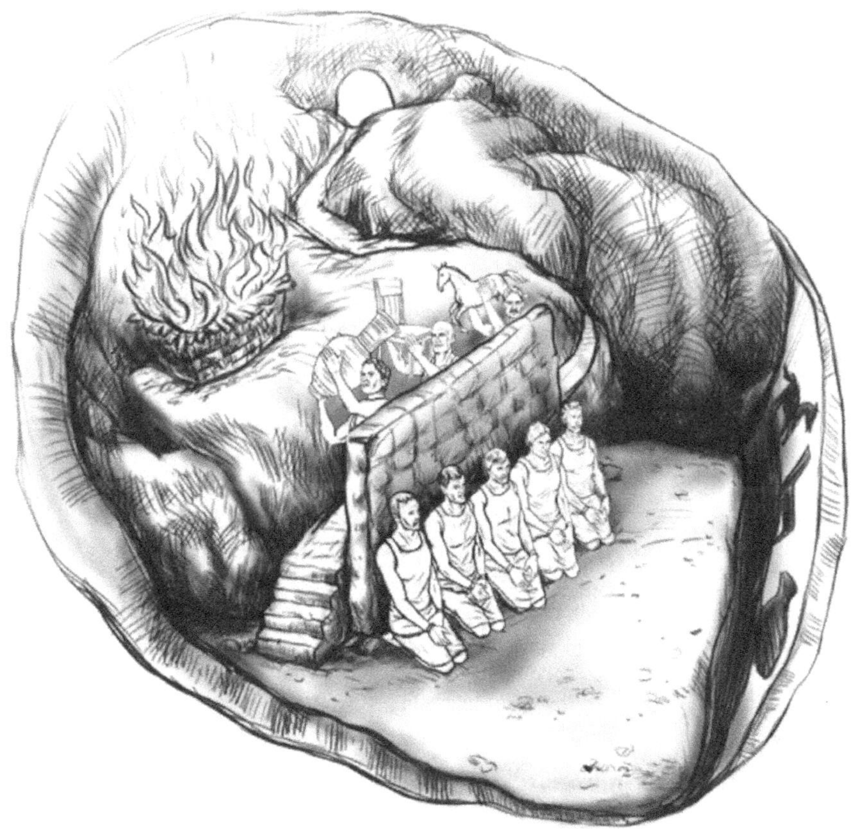

Figure 1: Plato's Cave

In the image, we see fire projecting shadows on the wall within the cave. Prisoners, bound by chains, face the wall with the shadows. The prisoners cannot move and have never seen anything other than

22 Plato, *Republic*, [514-515], 388.

the shadows before them. Since the shadows are all that they have ever known, they have become convinced that the shadows are all that exist. In the allegory, the shadows represent the world of sensory perception to which you and I are currently confined. Since all we have ever seen is shifting shadows—a changing, material world—we often mistake those shadows for reality. Yet the philosopher uses the mind's eye to venture outside the cave of sensation to the real world of unchanging absolutes. The body is chained inside the cave but the soul is free to venture outside. We escape the physical world of sensation to discover an unchanging realm of thought.

Plato was quick to point out that many of the concepts we encounter in mathematics seem far superior to what we experience in physical reality. Take the equation "1=1" as it appears printed on this page. At first glance, the first and second instance of the number "1" probably appear identical, but if you take out a magnifying glass, you will see some subtle differences between the two. The ink (or pixels) will undoubtedly have subtle smudges and imperfections. If you take out your microscope, the differences between the two "1s" will seem monstrous. Of course, it is self-evident that 1=1. This is called the "law of identity" in formal logic, and the "reflexive property" of numbers in mathematics. However, you will never find two "1s" that are perfectly identical in the material world. If you look close enough, there will be differences. Bertrand Russell, in his *History of Western Philosophy*, describes the situation as follows:

> Geometry deals with exact circles, but no sensible object is exactly circular; however carefully we may use our compasses, there will be some imperfections and irregularities. This suggests the view that all exact reasoning applies to ideal as opposed to sensible objects; it is natural to go further, and to argue that thought is nobler than

> sense, and the objects of thought more real than those of sense-perception.[23]

Plato surmised that the intellectual world is superior to the material world because the intellectual world of the soul is akin to the unchanging realm of Forms or Ideas. In the soul, we find grade school concepts such as perfectly straight lines that stretch on infinitely, which we could never hope to discover through sensory perception. In the world of sensation we find relative beauty, relative equality, relative truth, but Plato argued that we find these things in their essence, pure and unchanging, simple and indivisible, in the Realm of Forms.

Plato extended his Theory of Ideas beyond such lofty concepts as love, truth, justice, numbers, etc., to include even ordinary things such as beds and tables.[24] This helped Plato to explain how we are able to identify beds of all different sorts *as beds*. For we can easily imagine beds of various heights and sizes in practically infinite configurations. Whatever definition of a "bed" we give, we are bound to discover a bed somewhere that doesn't quite match our definition. If we say that a bed is a soft place to sleep, a bed of nails will provide an exception. Yet every bed must surely have something in common or else the word would be meaningless. The word "bed" must seemingly point to an enduring reality beyond itself. According to Plato, we identify a bed as a bed because it participates in the Ideal Form of a bed.[25] There is one single, simple, immutable, ideal bed, and every material, transitory bed that we encounter in the physical world is identified as a bed because we have in our soul some knowledge of the ideal bed in the unchanging realm.

It would be a mistake to imagine that the Realm of Forms is a material place in some physical location, for Plato likens it more to the

---

23 Russell, *History*, 37.

24 Plato, *Republic*, [596], 427.

25 Plato, *Republic*, [597], 428.

soul and human thoughts.[26] Even so, the cave allegory strongly suggests that the Realm of Forms is not just an actual, existent place, but a *more actual, existent* place than the physical world that you and I currently occupy. Plato's Realm of Forms is an immaterial, heavenly place. Plato's conception seems to have a great deal of affinity with the Christian conception of a spirit world of invisible principalities. It is easy to overlook the fact that, historically considered, Plato was instrumental in popularizing the conception of a spiritual plane of reality.

According to Plato, we discover unchanging truth by leaving the illusory world of change behind and by entering a world of pure thought. To meditate on unchanging truth is to step out of the cave of sensation and into the unchanging Realm of Forms. In this way, the philosopher walks toward the light of pure *being*:

> The true lover of knowledge is always striving after being—that is his nature; he will not rest in the multiplicity of individuals which is an appearance only, but will go on—the keen edge will not be blunted, nor the force of his desire abate until he have attained the knowledge of the true nature of every essence by a sympathetic and kindred power in the soul, and by that power drawing near and mingling and becoming incorporate with very being, having begotten mind and truth, he will have knowledge and will live and grow truly, and then, and not till then, will he cease from his travail.[27]

---

26 It is sometimes said that Plato's Realm of Ideals is "abstract," but this is incorrect inasmuch as something abstract exists only in the mind. Plato's demand is that every intramental reality (i.e., every notion inside the mind) has some extramentally real object that it corresponds to in the Realm of Forms. We recognize beauty in particular instances only on account of the eternally timeless Form of beauty that rests within our soul. Behind every concept stands an eternal "essence" in the Realm of Forms.

27 Plato, *Republic*, [490], 376.

How does changing man come about this unchanging knowledge of the Forms? Borrowing from various Greek religious and philosophical traditions, Plato surmised that we have an innate knowledge of the eternal Forms because we are caught up in an endless cycle of transmigration, more popularly known as reincarnation. We have each visited the Realm of Forms countless times before and we retain some knowledge of that realm. The immortal soul, which has always existed, has some "recollection" of it.[28] In fact, when we learn new concepts, it's not that we conjure new notions out of thin air; rather, we simply recall what we forgot when our eternal soul was transplanted into our current body.

Full of unchanging and heavenly ideas, the philosopher's soul (unlike that of the carnally minded man) is light and airy and, upon death, naturally ascends back to the unchanging realm which is more akin to the gods.[29] According to Plato, salvation is through philosophy. It is not that heaven must be incarnated on earth; rather, earth must conjure heaven within itself.

According to Plato, all human passions—all physical and emotional pains and pleasures—are unhelpful and unproductive because they serve only to remind us that we exist in a changing, misleading physical body:

> Each pleasure and pain is a sort of nail which nails and rivets the soul to the body, until she becomes like the body, and believes that to be true which the body affirms to be true; and from agreeing with the body and having the same delights she is obliged to have the same habits and haunts, and is not likely ever to be pure at her departure to the world below [i.e., Hades, the afterlife], but is always infected by body; and so she sinks into another body and

---

28 Plato, *Phaedo*, [75], 230.

29 Plato, *Phaedo*, [80], 232.

> there germinates and grows, and has therefore no part in the communion of the divine and pure and *simple*.[30]

Physical pain and changing emotional states draw us away from the all-important business of unbiased intellectual contemplation of the simple, divine Forms. For Plato, physical pain and pleasure is bad because our physical needs and desires drag us back down to the physical world. Our emotional changes stunt reposed intellectual contemplation, thereby dragging us back down into the cave of shadows. The soul of the good man is free from emotions and more like the impassible, unchanging Realm of Forms. The philosopher is suited to a higher, static mode of being as he consciously forsakes his physicality and gives himself over to the contemplation of simple, static, unchanging Forms.

The highest knowledge the philosopher attains is the knowledge of what Plato calls "the Good."[31] It is a mistake to think that human terminology can properly apply to the Good because it is transcendent beyond predication, words, and human concepts.[32] The Good "exceeds essence in dignity and power."[33] The Good is above and beyond existence as we know it. The Good is too high, too exalted, too transcendent to be known by finite man. Plato's "Good" is seemingly impersonal; that's certainly how his successors understood him, at any rate. For Plato, the Good is not identical to God; rather, the Good is a higher reality than God. For Plato, God is far from absolute; God is subordinate to the Good, subject to the Fates, co-equal with the eternal Forms.

God is said to be the author of only good things and bad cannot be attributed to him.[34] The Demiurge is a "God perfectly *simple* and true both in word and deed; *he changes not*; he deceives not, either by

30 Plato, *Phaedo*, [83], 234.

31 Plato, *Republic*, [517], 389.

32 see Plato, *7th letter*, see Copleston, *History*, V1, 179.

33 Plato, *Republic*, [509], 386.

34 Plato, *Republic*, [379], 322.

sign or word, by dream or waking vision."[35] According to Plato, then, God is simple, immutable, and impassible. Plato admits that much of this information is conjecture—mere opinion and not true knowledge—for the subject matter is difficult and knowledge of such things difficult to attain.

We will examine some of the difficulties that Plato's philosophy faced in the next chapter. I conclude this chapter simply by noting that Plato clearly possessed a mind of the first rank. His work serves as a powerful reminder in every age that absolute truth is absolutely necessary if human thought has any enduring value. The outstanding Jesuit historian of Philosophy, Frederick Copleston (1907–1994), speaks well to this point:

> Whatever imperfections or errors there may be in his Theory of Ideas, we must never forget that Plato meant to establish ascertained truth. He firmly held that we can, and do, apprehend essences in thought, and he firmly held that these essences are not purely subjective creations of the human mind (as though the ideal of justice, for instance, were purely man's creation and relative in character): we do not create them, we discover them. We judge of things according to standards, whether moral and aesthetic standards or generic and specific types: all judgment necessarily implies such standards, and if the scientific judgment is objective, then these standards must have objective reference. But they are not found, and cannot be found, in the sense-world as such: therefore they must be transcendent of the fleeting world of sense-particulars.[36]

Undoubtedly, Plato had many sound intuitions. Not every pagan idea is false, of course, and my argument is certainly not that we should

35 Plato, *Republic*, [382], 324.

36 Copleston, *History*, V1, 203.

reject an idea just because Plato said it. I have no interest in waging a smear campaign against a long dead philosopher. I think we can all understand and appreciate some of the reasons why the early church saw Plato as an ally and friend.

3

Plato's Self-Refutation

IT remains a credit to a great mind that Plato left us a forceful criticism of his own theory later in his life, in the opening pages of the dialogue *Parmenides*. He was both humble and honest enough to admit that he had a great deal of indecisiveness about his Theory of Ideas, and that many questions remained unanswered. An ideal, unchanging, perfect *justice* sounds plausible; an ideal, unchanging, perfect *bed*, less so. Does every word in our vocabulary have some real point of reference in the Realm of Forms? Is there an Ideal Form of mud and filth and excrement? Plato was unsure:

> I sometimes get disturbed, and begin to think that there is nothing without an idea; but then again, when I have taken up this position, I run away, because I am afraid that I may fall into a bottomless pit of nonsense, and perish; and so I return to the ideas of which I was just now speaking [the beautiful and the good], and occupy myself with them.[1]

1 Plato, *Parmenides*, [130], 488. Socrates is the speaker, but it's obviously Plato's view being expressed.

Though the Theory of Ideas was intended to save intellectual truth from endless change—to save epistemology from ontological decay—and thus to help us make sense of the world, it seemed as if that simple and time-less realm was in danger of becoming just as complicated as this world of change. In short, the theory seems to run the risk of creating more problems than it actually solves.

Plato also admitted that he wasn't entirely sure what it meant for a material thing to "participate" in an unchanging Form. The manner and mode of participation remained very hazy. Relative terms such as "greatness" and "likeness" were particularly troublesome. For example, Plato examined the idea of "smallness." He imagined that every particular thing that we identify as "small" is recognized as such because it participates in the eternal, unchanging Form of smallness, that is, in the Form of the perfectly, absolutely, time-lessly small.

Yet, in most cases, the thing described as small—say, a small bed—will not be absolutely small but only relatively small. It is smaller than other beds, but not the smallest bed imaginable. It seems that since the small bed in question is not absolutely small, it does not participate in all of the absolute smallness. This presented several problems. For one, since the small bed in question is not absolutely small, but only relatively small, it seemingly possesses only a portion of the absolute smallness. This portion of the absolute smallness would seemingly be smaller than the absolutely small, but that is absurd.[2]

Plato repeatedly emphasized that the Forms are simple and indivisible. It is, after all, preposterous to suppose that the Form of absolute indivisibility could be divisible.[3] Likewise, you cannot divide the

2 Plato, *Parmenides*, [131], 489. Plato's argument here seems to be based, in part, on a semantic equivocation, by which the same word is used in two different ways, which is very common in the writings of Plato and in ancient Greek philosophy in general.

3 See Plato, *Parmenides*, [131], 488. Plato certainly hints at the idea, though he does not state it explicitly.

absolutely small into smaller components. By definition, Plato's Forms have no parts. The Form of the absolutely small cannot be divided up into smaller parts, for it is not built up out of parts in the first place. At the same time, however, it seems obvious that no material thing can be absolutely small. All physical material can theoretically be divided into smaller portions. It seems impossible to allow that the entire Form of absolute smallness could participate in any particular material thing. Yet it seemed equally impossible that the Form of absolute smallness could be used in any sort of *partial* way, for it has no parts to begin with.

Plato admitted that it seemed impossible to divide the simple Forms, and equally impossible to suppose that the whole Form participated in a material thing.[4] Absolute, unchanging, simple essences cannot exist in us in their entirety or else they would no longer be simple and absolute.[5] Plato seemed to be stuck with a compatibility problem, whereby the Forms are simple and time-less, but we are neither.

Plato momentarily entertained the notion that perhaps the Forms exist only in the mind (thus anticipating later developments), but quickly dismissed this option. Plato reasoned that every thought is a thought about *something*, for, strictly speaking, it is impossible to think something about nothing. If my thought cannot be about nothing, then it must be about something, but every *something* can only be identified *as a something* by participating in an unchanging Form. This argument seems very circular and is not very compelling to the modern reader, but Plato accepted it.

According to Plato, every word and concept directs our attention to some unchanging Form. When I see a bed, I am able to identify it as a bed because I have some prior knowledge of the Ideal bed in the Realm of Forms. Without the Form of a bed—the bed essence—"attaching"

---

4 Plato, *Parmenides*, [131], 489

5 see Plato, *Parmenides*, [133], 489-490.

itself, in some manner, to every particular bed, we could not have a unified idea about what a bed is.[6]

This brings us to Plato's most forceful argument against his Theory of Ideas, the so-called third man argument:

> In my opinion, the ideas are, as it were, patterns fixed in nature, and other things are like them, and resemblances of them—what is meant by the participation of others in the ideas, is really assimilation to them.
>
> But if, said [Parmenides], the individual is like the idea, must not the idea also be like the individual, in so far as the individual is a resemblance of the idea? That which is like, cannot be conceived of as other than the like of like.
>
> Impossible.
>
> And when two things are alike, must they not partake of the same idea?
>
> They must.
>
> And will not that of which the two partake, and which makes them alike, be the idea itself?
>
> Certainly.
>
> Then the idea cannot be like the individual, or the individual like the idea; for if they are alike, some further idea of likeness will always be coming to light, and if that be like anything else, another; and the new ideas will be always arising, if the idea resembles that which partakes of it?
>
> Quite true.

6 Plato, *Parmenides*, [132], 489.

> The theory, then, that other things participate in the ideas by resemblance, has to be given up, and some other mode of participation devised?
>
> It would seem so.[7]

The argument can be expressed several ways. In simplest terms, if we suppose that each man we meet participates in the Form of the ideal, unchanging, perfect man, and, further, that each man we encounter bears this "likeness" or "similarity" to every other man we meet, then a new Form of "similarity" has entered the picture. Yet this contradicts Plato's intention of having only one Form that corresponds to each object we encounter in the physical world. Each man we meet will need to participate in a multitude of Forms. Each man will have the Form of child or adult, the Form of handsome or ugly, the Form of employed or unemployed, the Form of educated or uneducated, and so on.

If we discover other things that bear a "likeness" or "similarity" to one another (say, two horses), presumably the Form "similarity" is situated above both the unchanging Form of man and above the unchanging Form of horse. It seems to place us in an infinite regress wherein super-Forms will be situated in an infinite hierarchy over top of the more common Forms. Far from simplifying intellectual thought, the Theory of Ideas seems, at this point, to have placed us in a far worse predicament.

Plato hinted at other problems. Do changing things participate in the unchanging Form of change? Does time have a time-less Form? Do multiplicity and division possess Forms which are simple and indivisible? More significantly, how are the unchanging Forms compatible with minds that are always changing? How can that which is pure

---

7 Plato, *Parmenides*, [132-133], 489. The name of the argument—the third man—is derived from Aristotle's adaptation of the argument as found in the *Metaphysics*, where Aristotle uses the example of the Ideal man, much as I have done in the exposition to follow.

becoming be made compatible with that which is pure *being*? Our minds are not simple and time-less like the unchanging Forms; rather, they are *composite* and *in time*.

Central to Plato's philosophy is the notion that reality has two layers or modes. Plato's *two modes of being* can be illustrated as follows:

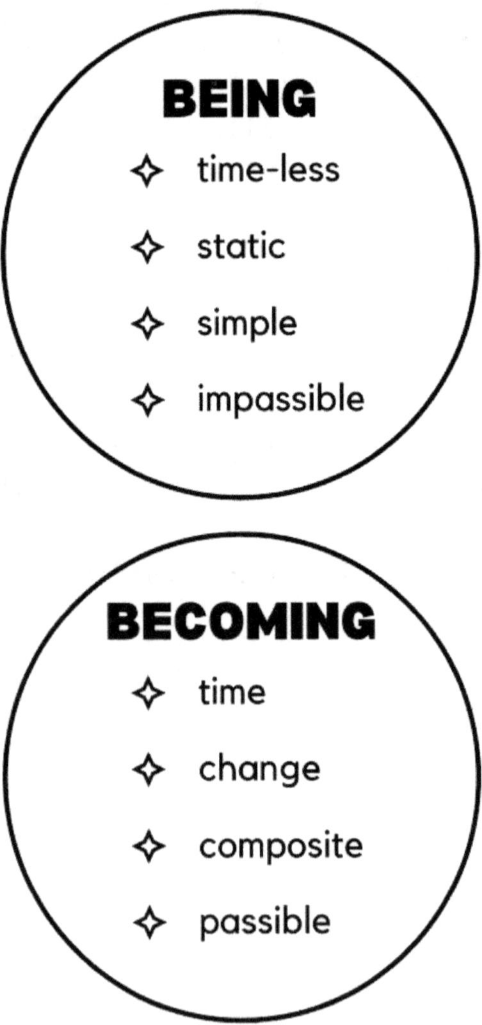

Figure 2: The Platonic Divorce

The bottom sphere is the world we live in, our realm of time and succession, our cave of shadows. Everything in this realm is constantly changing; all is subject to moth and rust and passions. The upper sphere is Plato's unchanging Realm of Forms. That realm is static and timeless, motionless and impassible. It is absolutely unchanging, always identical to itself, immovably at one with itself.

Yet this sort of bifurcation of reality into two modes of being—seemingly antithetical to one another—entailed serious epistemological difficulties. We operate in time and all of the facts we know have direct reference to time. None of our life experiences is time-less in the strict, philosophical sense. How can this world of time be compatible with that time-less world? A time-less mind would seemingly struggle to think in terms of time, just as our time-bound minds are incapable of forming a clear conception of what it would be like to think time-lessly.

The case of simplicity is similar. Human knowledge is all about defining distinct terms and making clear distinctions between various concepts. Human thought is manifold and complex. How could our manifold, non-simple minds ever come to grips with simple, distinctionless realities?

To be "simple" in the philosophical sense of the word is to be strictly uniform and indivisible. Ancient philosophers used the term "simple" similar to the way we use the word "homogeneous." When I buy a gallon of homogenized milk at the grocery store, I understand that I am buying a gallon of milk in which the consistency is all the same. The milk, cream, and butter will not separate inside the jug. The milk is simple and not composite as far as the naked eye is concerned. It is all the same stuff inside and will not admit of any internal division or separation. From beginning to end, it is one and the same as itself, and it is only one thing. As far as the naked eye is concerned, it is all milk and just milk such that no distinctions can be found within it.

However, human thought is not simple; it is built out of countless distinct parts, concepts, notions, assumptions, impressions, etc. So too human language consists of numerous letters, syllables, sentences, paragraphs, sounds, and utterances. We cannot think or speak in simple terms, so how could our non-simple minds ever come to grips with simple truths? Plato's two realms thus strike us as *divorced* from one another such that they would be unknowable to one another. Copleston highlights the force of this objection:

> The objection is also raised that on Socrates' theory the Ideas would be unknowable. Man's knowledge is concerned with the objects of this world, and with the relations between individual objects. We can, for example, know the relation between the individual master and the individual slave, but this knowledge is insufficient to inform us as to the relationship between absolute mastership (the Idea of Mastership) and absolute slavery (the Idea of Slavery). For that purpose we should require absolute knowledge and this we do not possess. This objection, too, shows the hopelessness of regarding the Ideal World as merely parallel to this world: if we are to know the former, then there must be some objective basis in the latter which enables us to know it. If the two worlds are merely parallel, then, just as we would know the sensible world without being able to know the Ideal World, so a divine intelligence would know the Ideal World without being able to know the sensible world.[8]

Plato seems to be stuck with an acute breakdown of communication between two *polar opposite* modes of being. The two realms have been defined in such a way that they wholly exclude one another. Time and time-lessness literally have nothing in common; *they wholly exclude one another, by definition*. The same is true of simplicity; not only would we be incapable of knowing anything about that simple

---

8 Copleston, *History,* V1, 183.

realm, but neither could any being in that simple realm know anything about this manifold, non-simple realm.

Thus, in the diagram above, there is no overlap between the two spheres, no point of connection or contact. Time-lessness is strictly incompatible with time. Immutability is strictly incompatible with change. Simplicity is strictly incompatible with our world of manifold complexity. Thus we discover an unbridgeable canyon of epistemic separation, two diametrically opposed modes of being or ways of existing. In short, we cannot think in time-less or simple terms; such a feat is impossible for us. This epistemological separation inherent to the Platonic philosophy shall be referred to as the *Platonic Divorce.*

The antithesis between two contrary—seemingly opposing—modes of being became the central problem of subsequent ancient and medieval philosophy. Early Christian thinkers wholeheartedly embraced the premise that God's mode of being is antithetical to our own, and thus failed to recognize the problem as a distinctly *Platonic* problem. They were left with the same profound isolation problem, whereby man cannot think in divine terms, and God cannot think in human terms. We will see this theme recur in every subsequent thinker in this volume.

Now every student of classical Greek philosophy knows that the ancient Greeks tended to be dualistic in the sense that they constantly asserted the real existence of antithetical, binary pairs. This bias can be seen in nearly all ancient Greek philosophical thought. Light was thought to be the binary opposite of dark, matter the binary opposite of soul, good the binary opposite of evil, and so on. Since the two were related as binaries, the existence of one half of the pair seemed, in each case, to suggest the necessary existence of the other half. "Harmony," in the Greek sense of the term, is achieved when neither of the opposing forces is dominant over the other, and the two exist in steady equilibrium with everything in its proper place. One does not need to look very hard to spot this tendency in ancient Greek philosophy.

From a modern, Protestant perspective, none of the above propositions is true, however. Physical darkness is simply the absence of light. Evil is failing to do that which is morally acceptable. The existence of good does not, in any way, necessitate the existence of evil. Matter and soul are distinguished from one another, but they're hardly antithetical. This faulty Greek dualism of antithetical, binary pairs can also be seen in some of the Hellenistic works of the Apocrypha, such as in the Book of Sirach:

> All things come in pairs, one opposite
> the other,
> And he has made nothing
> incomplete. (42:24)

And again:

> Good is the opposite of evil,
> and life the opposite of death;
> So the sinner is the opposite of the godly. (33:14)

Some early church "fathers," such as Jerome, rejected the canonicity of Sirach, but thinkers such as Clement of Alexandria and Augustine regarded the book as canonical.[9] For them, this Greek dualism of binary pairs was seemingly sanctioned by Scripture itself, and the acceptance of the Platonic dualism of antithetical opposites would have seemed all the more natural.

I would argue that Greek dualism lies at the root of the concepts of time-lessness, simplicity, immutability, and impassibility. Timelessness was imagined to be the antithesis of time, a world in which time played no part. Simplicity was imagined to be the antithesis of this world of aggregate complexity, a world in which nothing is aggregated or compounded, manifold or complex. Immutability was imagined to

---

9 See e.g., Augustine, *On Christian Doctrine*, 2.13 (721).

be the antithesis of change and flux, a world in which all is static, still, and motionless. Impassibility was imagined to be the complete absence of any sort of emotional or physical pull or inclination.

When God is defined as time-less, simple, and immutable, God becomes divorced from us, as our practical antithesis. We will see that it was always easy to infer the conclusion: a God *like that* cannot be known by the likes of us.

4

CLEMENT OF ALEXANDRIA

TODAY, the intellectual stature of Plato and his brightest student, Aristotle (384–322 BC), are generally regarded as equal. Historically, however, the works of Plato enjoyed vastly greater success. Aristotle's writing failed to capture the ancient imagination to the same extent as Plato. Plato was undoubtedly a more compelling writer, and his works were better suited to capture the ancient religious spirit. By the second century AD, even Aristotle's own school was teaching the doctrines of Platonism.[1]

Both thinkers were well known in the Greek-speaking world, but as Latin usurped Greek's role as the international language in western Europe, especially after the third century AD, the works of Aristotle had a much smaller circulation. His general outlook was not as amenable to Christianity as that of Plato. As one historian noted, "Aristotle, who was deemed to have taught that the world was eternal and to have denied divine providence as well as the immortality of the soul, seemed too much of a pagan."[2]

1 Copleston, *History*, V1, 427.

2 Luscombe, *Medieval*, 16-17.

Through most of the Middle Ages, only two of Aristotle's works on logic were available in translation. None of his other philosophical writings had been translated into Latin, and very few scholars were able to read ancient Greek. Aristotle was thus known as a figure of peripheral importance. His philosophical works fell into obscurity in Europe until the twelfth century AD when they were re-discovered and became the object of renewed academic zeal.

Platonism, on the other hand, gained ascendency for a millennia and a half. Its influence on Christian theology—still in its infancy—is incalculable. This influence is particularly acute among Eastern, Greek-speaking theologians like Clement of Alexandria and Dionysius the Areopagite (chapter 7). The influence of Platonism in the Latin West was moderated by the natural language barrier, as well as the Roman distaste for abstract—seemingly impractical—philosophical thought. Even so, there was no corner of ancient or medieval theology that was not heavily influenced by the writings of Plato and his successors. Copleston offers this general assessment:

> As a rough generalization, therefore, one may say that the philosophic ideas of the early Christian writers were Platonic or neo-Platonic in character (with an admixture of Stoicism) and that the Platonic tradition continued for long to dominate Christian thought from the philosophic viewpoint.[3]

Platonism offered great appeal to early Christians, and not without reason. As we have seen, Plato defended the idea of absolute truth against the skeptics of his day. Christians found themselves forced to do the same. Plato argued that the greatest truths could not be discovered by physical sensations; rather, we have to look beyond the physical in order to see the spiritual and immaterial. Christians similarly argued that we must exercise trust in the invisible God in order to effectively

---

3 Copleston, *History*, V2, 14.

wage war against the invisible principalities and powers of darkness. Platonists and Christians alike made a sharp distinction between the physical body and the immaterial soul. Christians found in Plato a powerful advocate against the crass materialism that often dominated the Roman world. Plato also argued for high moral standards founded upon objective and eternal truths, and here again Christians found an ally in an exceedingly violent, unethical era.

Many of the early church fathers were firmly convinced that Plato had played an instrumental role in priming the world for Christ's teachings. That they were correct in this judgment would, I think, be difficult to deny. Plato taught the world to look to an invisible, spiritual realm for truth. Even through most of the Old Testament, a great deal of emphasis had been placed on the physical and external. The one who touched a dead body, for instance, was deemed unfit to enter into God's presence until they had completed ceremonial washing and waited a sufficient amount of time (see Numbers 19:11). According to the author of Hebrews, all those old Levitical and ceremonial rules "relate only to food, drink, and various washings, regulations for the body imposed until a time of reformation" (Hebrews 9:10). In emphasizing the importance of invisible realities, Plato had undoubtedly done some work in readying the world for Christ's worldwide reformation.

Even so, an unrestrained zeal for Plato among early Christian scholars led to a great many excesses. This is evident in the works of Titus Flavius Clemens (c.150–c. 215 AD), better known as Clement of Alexandria. Clement was a Christian philosopher and theologian who taught at the Catechetical School of Alexandria, the single most important Christian educational institution in the second century. He was an influential apologist during an age of intense persecution against Christians. He reported that "we have exhibited before our eyes every day abundant sources of martyrs that are burnt, impaled, beheaded. All these...[are] trained so as to manifest their piety by their blood."[4]

Three of Clement's major works have survived the flux, along with a number of fragments. For our present purposes, the most important work, by far, is the *Miscellanies* in which Clement lays out his view of ancient Greek philosophy alongside an introduction to the "true philosophy" of Christianity. Here we will mostly concern ourselves with Clement's views regarding the compatibility of Christianity and Platonism and his doctrines of classical theism.

Though many Christians had suggested that philosophy was useless worldly wisdom, Clement argued that this view was an oversimplification. *Philo-sophia* is, literally, the "love of wisdom." Philosophy is the principled use of natural reason. To refute philosophy one must inevitably appeal to human rationality. Thus, for Clement, to refute philosophy is still to utilize philosophy.[5]

According to Clement, many of the conclusions of philosophy are supported by Scripture, and vice versa, and thus we can see that reason and revelation both lead in the same direction, namely, toward the attainment of absolute truth. "The way of truth is therefore one. But into it, as into a perennial river, streams flow from all sides."[6] Philosophy is the use of our God-given natural ability to reason, and thus, "philosophy is in a sense a work of Divine Providence."[7]

Clement was the first to argue that philosophy is the "handmaiden" of theology. Though Plato and his peers obtained true and genuine insights through the use of the natural powers of reasoning, their systems were incomplete. For Clement, Christian faith represented the final stage and end goal of philosophical thought. He had no shortage of metaphors to describe this harmonious relation. Where

---

4 Clement, *Miscellanies*, II.XX.

5 Clement, *Miscellanies*, I.II.

6 Clement, *Miscellanies*, I.V.

7 Clement, *Miscellanies*, I.I.

Christian truth is the dinner, philosophy is the dessert. Where Christ is a fertile field producing fruit, philosophy is the wall of defense surrounding it.[8]

Clement placed little emphasis on man's noetic or intellectual depravity. His view, rather, is that the best of the Greeks pursued the truth with honesty and integrity no less than the best of the Hebrews. Moses, Plato, and Paul all loved the same truth and were all philosophers of the one, true type. Acceptance of Christianity was not seen by Clement as the renovation of one's entire outlook, but simply as the consummation of a worldview that was already basically on the right track.[9]

Clement was astonished by the profound insight of the Greek philosophers. He even went so far as to suggest the possibility that they received supernatural insight directly from God. Clement said it could be the case that the Stoics, Pythagoreans, and Plato wrote by "the inspiration of God."[10] Plato is cited as having recognized that there were "prophets" among the Greeks, and Clement assumed that the Greek and Hebrew notions of prophecy were, for all intents and purposes, identical.[11] He said that the "truth-loving Plato" spoke "as if divinely inspired."[12] Plato even spoke "prophetically" of the coming Lord's day.[13] It should be noted, in fairness to Clement, that he was not dogmatic on this point. His language is tentative; he offered the hypothesis—almost always with a degree of hesitation—as a way to try to account for the seemingly inexplicable greatness of Greek philosophical insight.

Clement believed that Hebrew thought and Greek thought had borrowed from one another through the centuries and that no harm

---

8 Clement, *Miscellanies*, I.XX.

9 See Pelikan, *Christian Tradition*, 46.

10 Clement, *Exhortation*, VI.

11 See Clement, *Miscellanies*, I.XV.

12 Clement, *Miscellanies*, I.VIII.

13 Clement, *Miscellanies*, V.XIV.

had been done to either because both sought the attainment of the same system of truth. For example, Clement argued that Moses learned Greek philosophy while living with Pharaoh's daughter in Egypt.[14] In reality, this view is highly anachronistic; formal philosophy didn't exist until at least half a millennium after Moses' death. We can forgive Clement, of course, for not having the resources available to fully appreciate this chronology.

According to Clement, the Apostle Paul likewise gave his nod of approval to much of the Greek tradition by quoting Aratus (e.g., in Acts 17:28) and other Greek poets favorably.[15] Clement assumed that Paul quoted the Greek poets with a general sense of approval of their methods and systems of thought.

Likewise, Clement suggested that the Greeks cheated a bit in attaining their profound knowledge of God. He argued that the Persian king, Artaxerxes (presumably the Artaxerxes I mentioned in the biblical book of Ezra), translated the Old Testament Scriptures and that the Pythagoreans, Socrates, and Plato "derived a great deal from this source."[16] However, nowhere in classical Greek philosophy do we find any mention of Moses or the Hebrew Scriptures. Clement believed this was a sustained and concerted act of dishonesty; though the Greeks plagiarized and pilfered their best ideas about God from the Hebrews, in an act of unfaithfulness, they failed to acknowledge the original source. According to Clement, "The philosophers of the Greeks are called thieves, inasmuch as they have taken without acknowledgment their principal dogmas from Moses and the prophets."[17]

Clement's argument that the Greeks stole their "principal dogmas" about God from the Hebrews was used to bolster his argument that Greek philosophy and biblical theology taught a very similar set of

---

14 Clement, *Miscellanies*, I.XXIII.

15 Clement, *Miscellanies*, I.XIX.

16 Clement, *Miscellanies*, I.XXII. See also V.XIV.

17 Clement, *Miscellanies*, V.I.

truths about God. The idea that Plato pilfered his best ideas from Moses offered an easy explanation for the alleged agreement between the two. Of Plato, he writes:

> You have learned geometry from the Egyptians, astronomy from the Babylonians; the charms of healing you have got from the Thracians; the Assyrians also have taught you many things; but for the laws that are consistent with truth, and your sentiments respecting God, you are indebted to the Hebrews…[18]

The notion that ancient Greek philosophers—particularly Plato—borrowed various ideas about God from Hebrew thought was already present among the Jews in the days of Christ. It is a prevalent theme of the Jewish philosopher, Philo of Alexandria (20 BC–c. 50 AD), for example, who used this thesis for apologetic purposes similar to those of Clement.[19]

However commonplace, this type of argument now seems little more than an extended act of wishful thinking on the part of Jewish and early Christian theologians. There is no evidence in the writings of Plato that he had any knowledge of the Hebrew Scriptures. We now know that the Greeks were largely isolated from outside sources until about a century after Plato's death. Nor is there any evidence to support the theory that the Persian kings in the biblical era translated the Old Testament. The translation of the Old Testament into Greek (called the LXX or Septuagint) was at the request of Ptolemy II Philadelphus (285–247 BC), who was born some six decades after Plato's death.[20]

---

18 Clement, *Exhortation*, VI.

19 For a fuller account, see Pelikan, *Christian Tradition*, 33.

20 Even if the Persian kings had made a Persian translation of Scripture, it's not exactly clear what use it would have been to Plato. The Persians spoke Persian where the Greeks, as it turns out, spoke Greek.

Clement frequently overlooked important differences between Platonic and Hebrew conceptions of reality. Oftentimes, he is guilty of reading Platonic doctrines *into* Scripture and then of accusing Plato of having stolen the doctrine in question. Pelikan's view, on this point, is undoubtedly correct:

> It is, of course, true that many of the ideas that seemed so similar to philosophical teachings were being read into the Old Testament rather than being found there; for example, Clement's doctrine of creation in some ways owed more to Plato than to Moses, even though he claimed to find that doctrine in the latter rather than in the former and had to explain the embarrassing parallel.[21]

Clement theorized that God used philosophy as preparation for salvation for the Greeks, much like he used the Hebrew Torah as preparation for salvation for the Hebrews. What the Law was to the Jews, so philosophy was to the Greeks:

> Perchance, too, philosophy was given to the Greeks directly and primarily, till the Lord should call the Greeks. For this was a schoolmaster to bring "the Hellenic mind," as the law, the Hebrews, "to Christ." Philosophy, therefore, was a preparation, paving the way for him who is perfected in Christ.[22]

Here again we find the suggestion that "perchance" the Greeks were given revelation of their philosophical systems "directly" from God. This would help to explain how the Greeks arrived at many of the same conclusions about God as the Hebrews. According to Clement, in the same way that the Law was a tutor for the Hebrews until Christ should appear (see, e.g. Galatians 3:24), so too philosophy was a tutor

21 Pelikan, *Christian Tradition*, 34.

22 Clement, *Miscellanies*, I.V.

for the Greeks. Clement's theory was that the Jews were justified by the Law of Moses until such time as Christ appeared, and so too the Greeks were justified by philosophy:

> Although at one time philosophy justified the Greeks, not conducting them to that entire righteousness to which it is ascertained to cooperate, as the first and second flight of steps help you in your ascent to the upper room...[23]

By the use of philosophy, then, the Greeks attained a high degree of righteousness, and their righteousness was essentially Christian in character. Philosophy was a vehicle of salvation for the Greeks: "Accordingly, before the advent of the Lord, philosophy was necessary to the Greeks for righteousness."[24]

How then was the Greek philosopher ultimately saved? Clement argued that though both the Greeks and Hebrews spent some time in purgatorial suffering after their death, Christ preached the gospel to both groups in the days that intervened between his death and resurrection. Those who were faithful in principle accepted the Lord's message and were finally saved. According to Clement, the Lord:

> preached the Gospel to those in Hades. For it was requisite, in my opinion, that as here, so also there, the best of the disciples should be imitators of the Master; so that He should bring to repentance those belonging to the Hebrews, and they the Gentiles: that is, those who had lived in righteousness according to the Law and Philosophy, who had ended life not perfectly, but sinfully.[25]

According to this theory, though neither the Hebrew Law nor Greek philosophy fully saved anyone, those Jews who abided by the Law

---

23 Clement, *Miscellanies*, I.XX.

24 Clement, *Miscellanies*, I.V.

25 Clement, *Miscellanies*, VI.VI.

along with those Greeks who abided by philosophy (who were each, therefore, faithful in principle to what they were given by God) were given another chance, after death, to accept faith in Jesus and receive full deliverance from their suffering. God is no respecter of persons, after all: "For, having furnished the one with the commandments, and the other with philosophy, He shut up unbelief to the Advent."[26]

> What then? Did not the same dispensation obtain in Hades, so that even there, all the souls, on hearing the proclamation, might either exhibit repentance, or confess that their punishment was just, because they believed not?[27]

Clement based his theory largely on 1 Peter 3:19 which speaks of Jesus making a proclamation to "spirits in prison."[28] The passage is very difficult and remains a matter of debate. Clement took the passage to mean that Jesus went to Hell for the short period that intervened between his death and resurrection, and preached the gospel to those in purgatorial torment.[29] According to Clement, this gave Jesus a chance to fully convert Plato and many other Greek philosophers.

In Clement's estimation, then, Greek philosophers like Plato could practically be thought of as immature Christians. In one place he wrote, "Philosophers, then, are children, unless they have been made men by Christ."[30] Plato and the rest were Christian believers in

---

26 Clement, *Miscellanies*, VII.II.

27 Clement, *Miscellanies*, VI.VI.

28 The mistranslation of "sheol" as "hell" in Psalm 16:10 in the LLX also certainly played a part. See also the Apocrypha, Wisdom of Solomon 16:13-14 which likens Hades to being "imprisoned."

29 The same teaching seems to appear in the Apostles Creed which says Jesus "descended into hell" after his death and before his resurrection. The Apostles Creed was beginning to take shape in Clement's day and seems to bear his influence in this regard. Augustine likewise taught that Jesus "descended in order to loose some from the chains of hell"(*The City of God*, 17.11 [527]).

30 Clement, *Miscellanies*, I.XI.

principle, no less than Moses or the prophets. Clement agreed with the rhetorical question posed by one of his peers: "For what is Plato, but Moses speaking in Attic Greek?"[31]

According to Clement, both Plato and Moses agreed about the Realm of Forms. In fact, Plato learned the theory from Moses: "For the region of God is hard to attain; which Plato called the region of ideas, having learned from Moses that it was a place which contained all things universally."[32] Clement described the basic thesis of Platonism as follows:

> In reasoning, it is possible to divine [i.e to intuit] respecting God, if one attempt without any of the senses, by reason, to reach what is individual [i.e., indivisible, simple]; and do not quit the sphere of existences, till, rising up to the things which transcend it, he apprehends by the intellect itself that which is good, moving in the very confines of the world of thought, according to Plato.[33]

Clement agreed with Plato as to the correctness of this method. This difficult task of intellectual ascent to God by way of pure rationality was, according to Clement, what Paul meant when he said that we see through a glass dimly.[34] In true Platonic fashion, Clement said that knowledge of God is best attained by contemplation of the unchanging Forms of thought: "Reason, the governing principle, remaining unmoved and guiding the soul, is called its pilot. For access to the Immutable is obtained by a truly immutable means."[35] The best way to approach the static God is by contemplation of the static Forms. According to Clement, Plato used this method to arrive at a true knowledge of the one, true God:

---

31 Clement, *Miscellanies*, I.XXII. "Attic" is the Athenian dialect of the Greek language.

32 Clement, *Miscellanies*, V.XI.

33 Clement, *Miscellanies,* V.XI.

34 Clement, *Miscellanies*, V.XI, referring to 1 Corinthians 13:12.

35 Clement, *Miscellanies*, II.XI.

> And let it not be this one man alone—Plato; but, O philosophy, hasten to produce many others also, who declare the only true God to be God, through His inspiration, if in any measure they have grasped the truth.[36]

Almost comically, Clement, at times, turns Plato into a Christian minister:

> "No one," says the Lord, "hath known the Father but the Son, and he to whom the Son shall reveal Him." This, then, is to be believed, according to Plato, though it is announced and spoken "without probable and necessary proofs," but in the Old and New Testaments.[37]

Clement clearly held Plato in the highest degree of honor, not far from the Apostle Paul and even Jesus himself. We find countless instances where he disregards context and offers an allegorical or metaphorical interpretation of Plato to force him into accord with Scripture. Where Plato refers generally to "spirits," for example, Clement takes this as a distinct reference to the biblical Satan.[38] Likewise, countless biblical passages are unnaturally forced to accord with Platonism.

According to Clement, Plato recognized the distinction between God the Father and God the Son, and acknowledged the Holy Trinity.[39] This is, once again, quite anachronistic; belief in the Trinity simply didn't exist prior to the incarnation of Christ several hundred years after Plato's death.[40]

---

36 Clement, *Exhortation*, VI.

37 Clement, *Miscellanies,* V.XIII.

38 Clement, *Miscellanies*, V.XIV.

39 Clement, *Miscellanies*, V.XIV.

40 As the great Princeton theologian, B.B. Warfield, pointed out, the Old Testament, on its own, never produced a Trinitarian theology. It was only with the addition of the greater light of the New Testament that it became quite easy—and even necessary—to see the Trinity frequently in the Old Testament.

Clement defined "impassibility" as no mere "moderation of passion," but rather, "the complete eradication of desire."[41] Thus, it is clear that, for Clement, an impassable state is a state in which one has no feelings or emotional inklings whatsoever. To be impassible is to have no emotional high points and no emotional low points. Even gladness and high spirits are passions that are excluded for the Christian.[42] Clement's impassible man is akin to the refined Stoic, unaffected by every outward circumstance.

It may be noted in passing that Stoicism combined a materialistic cosmology with a deterministic view of history. In turn, these doctrines encouraged a rigid ethic of tranquil impassibility. To put it very briefly, man is but a domino in a line, and his influence is limited to his own disposition. The Stoic stared inevitability in the eye, as it were, and refused to be moved emotionally, come what may. For Plato, impassibility was seen as assisting in the business of abstract contemplation. In Stoicism, impassibility is more a practical and ethical consideration. Both systems encouraged impassibility as the highest of ethical virtues among both gods and men. Certainly Plato had an influence upon Stoicism in this regard.

If a Christian eats, according to Clement, it should not be because he enjoys or desires the food, but only because he will die if he doesn't eat. Likewise, Christians should abstain from all pleasure, for pleasure is the "fuel of lust."[43] Likewise, sex is only for procreation, and should not be enjoyed. Likewise, to be subject to emotions or desires is to pronounce oneself "not yet pure."[44] That the ascetic and monkish spirit of the Middle Ages owed much to Plato is obvious. Indeed, without Plato the whole period would be unintelligible. Isolation from the world and from the pains and pleasures of life was to pave the way for unhindered intellectual contemplation of God.

41 Clement, *Miscellanies*, VI.IX.

42 Clement, *Miscellanies*, VI.IX.

43 Clement, *Miscellanies*, II.XX.

44 Clement, *Miscellanies*, VI.IX.

Clement likened our emotions to the powers of darkness to whom we should never succumb.[45] "To be subjected to passions, and to yield to them, is the extremest slavery; as to keep them in subjection is the only liberty."[46] When Christ commanded us to take up our cross (see Matthew 16:24), he meant that man must "crucify himself from the passions…For if you would loose, and withdraw, and separate (for this is what the cross means) your soul from the delight and pleasure that is in this life, you will possess…the looked-for hope."[47] Plato is cited on this point, for Plato said that pleasure nailed the body to the soul and inhibited reposed contemplation. Clement believed that Plato's reference to nails was a prophetic hint about the future crucifixion of Jesus.

Christian martyrs are "Those that are superior to Pleasure, who rise above the passions, who know what they do—the Gnostics who are greater than the world."[48] Clement's use of the term "Gnostic" should not be mistaken for the ancient Gnostic heresy, as Clement rejected the Gnostic heresy. "Gnosis" was simply the everyday Greek word for knowledge. By "Gnostic" he simply meant the intellectually-minded, mature Christian. Of course, Clement's view of what it meant to be a mature Christian was heavily influenced by Platonism.[49] Though Clement denied that the body, as such, is sinful, still he followed Plato in his practical rejection of the physical in favor of the intellectual:

> For the gnostic soul must be consecrated to the light, stript of the integuments of matter, devoid of the frivolousness of the body and of all the passions, which are acquired

45 Clement, *Miscellanies*, II.XX.

46 Clement, *Miscellanies*, II.XXIII.

47 Clement, *Miscellanies*, II.XX.

48 Clement, *Miscellanies*, II.XX.

49 Not unlike Gnosticism itself. With its strict physical asceticism, general denigration of matter, and imagined secret philosophical knowledge (*gnosis*), the Platonic influence upon the Gnostic heresy is obvious.

> through vain and lying opinions, and divested of the lusts of the flesh.[50]

Because Plato thought little of the physical body, several early Christian heresies took issue with the idea that God would assume a base physical body in the person of the Messiah. We find this tendency already at work in the New Testament; the Apostle John, especially, went to great lengths to stress Christ's physicality and to stamp out this error. Jesus was the one "we have seen with our eyes…and touched with our hands" (1 John 1:1).

For Clement, impassibility was one clear goal of the Christian ethic. "Now the sacrifice which is acceptable to God is unswerving abstraction [i.e., withdrawal] from the body and its passions."[51] The true gnostic "has reached a state of passionlessness, waiting to put on the divine image."[52] When Christians look to overcome all passions, they are following the example of Christ the "royal Word, the impassible man."[53]

> Our Instructor is like His Father God, whose son He is, sinless, blameless, and with a soul devoid of passion; God in the form of man… He is to us a spotless image; to Him we are to try with all our might to assimilate our souls. He is wholly free from human passions; wherefore also He alone is judge, because He alone is sinless. As far, however, as we can, let us try to sin as little as possible.[54]

To be passionless is to follow the example of Jesus and the Apostles:

---

50 Clement, *Miscellanies*, V.XI.

51 Clement, *Miscellanies*, V.XI.

52 Clement, *Miscellanies*, IV.XXII.

53 Clement, *Miscellanies*, V.XIV.

54 Clement, *Instructor*, I.II.

> But He [the Savior] was entirely impassible (*apathes*); inaccessible to any movement of feeling—either pleasure or pain. While the apostles, having most gnostically mastered, through the Lord's teaching, anger and fear, and lust, were not liable even to such of the movements of feeling, as seem good, courage, zeal, joy, desire, through a steady condition of mind, not changing a whit; but ever continuing unvarying in a state of training after the resurrection of the Lord.
>
> And should it be granted that the affections specified above, when produced rationally, are good, yet they are nevertheless inadmissible in the case of the perfect man, who is incapable of exercising courage: for neither does he meet what inspires fear, as he regards none of the things that occur in life as to be dreaded; nor can aught dislodge him from this—the love he has towards God. Nor does he need cheerfulness of mind...Nor does he consequently love any one with this common affection, but loves the Creator in the creatures. ...He is compelled to become like his Teacher in impassibility.[55]

Clement here imagined that the Apostles, following Jesus' example, overcame all passions, including even feelings of joy, fear, anger and courage. Not only does this contradict the New Testament in countless ways (we may recall, for example, Jesus' outrage over the Temple being turned into a den of thieves), but it evidences a strong streak of perfectionism in Clement.

According to Clement, Christ recognized no psychological or physical anguish even on the cross, because he followed the example of his Father. "God is impassible, free of anger, destitute of desire."[56] It is

---

55 Clement, *Miscellanies*, VI.IX.

56 Clement, *Miscellanies*, IV.XXIII.

"wrong to conceive of God as subject to passions."[57] When Scripture says that there is no darkness in God, it means no emotions.[58] Man's final state is to be a state devoid of all feeling: "For universally liability to feeling belongs to every kind of desire; and man, when deified purely into a passionless state, becomes a unit."[59] By "unit" Clement seems to have meant an indivisible, simple entity. Rid of all desire in an unchanging state, man becomes motionless, immutable, eternally still. Man becomes "deified" like God in his apathic quietude.

I must press the reader at this point, was it from Scripture or from pagan philosophy that Clement learned this doctrine of impassibility? The Apostle says to us, "Rejoice in the Lord always; again I will say, rejoice!" (Phillipians 4:4). Clement, on the other hand, insists that God does not rejoice and neither should we.

Clement likewise followed Plato in teaching that God is simple. He defined simplicity for us when he said that "by division we get back to what is simple and more elementary."[60] Simplicity is "the point which…is incapable of further division."[61] Simplicity is thus the point at which one can no longer divide. Thus, there are no divisions or distinctions to be made within God. God is properly atomic and indivisible.

According to Clement, God is "above both space and time, and qualities of objects. Wherefore neither is He at any time in a part, either as containing or as contained, either by limitation or by section."[62] Here Clement indicates that, on account of his simplicity, God is above "qualities" and thus has no qualities. Seemingly he meant that, on account of his simplicity, all of God's attributes are really one and the

---

57 Clement, Miscellanies, V.IV.

58 Clement, *I Peter*, I.V.

59 Clement, *Miscellanies*, IV.XXIII.

60 Clement, *Miscellanies*, VII.VI.

61 Clement, *Miscellanies*, VII.VI.

62 Clement, *Miscellanies*, II.II.

same such that he does not possess a plurality of attributes or qualities. (The reader will recall that the milk in the jug is all milk and only milk.) It certainly seems problematic, however, for theology to deny the validity of its own distinctions upon the subject of God. Contemporary theologian, R.T. Mullins, notes that "If conceptual distinctions cannot even be applied to a simple God, it would seem that Christian theology is a non-starter."[63]

Clement taught that as we engage in abstract thought, we become more immutable, impassible, and simple like God himself:

> When, therefore, he who partakes gnostically of this holy quality devotes himself to contemplation, communing in purity with the divine, he enters more nearly into the state of impassible identity, so as no longer to *have* science and possess knowledge, but to *be* science and knowledge.[64]

As we contemplate God, we become identical to our own knowledge, thus imitating God's simplicity. Seemingly, the contemplation of God is a process that transforms us into simple, indivisible, quality-less beings like God himself.

The difficulty with this view is that if we become the same simple stuff, so to speak, that God is, this would imply that we become God-stuff and, thus, that we become identical to God. We will see Plotinus work out this implication with great consistency in the next chapter. On account of this difficulty, Clement's view that man eventually becomes simple, was, for the most part, rejected by later Christian thinkers. His doctrine of impassibility was likewise greatly watered down.

Clement defined "eternity" as the simultaneity of all time.[65] God sees all time all at once, simultaneously. God has no past or future that is not always present. Thus, God has no past and no future, as

63 Mullins, *Simply Impossible*, 185.

64 Clement, *Miscellanies*, IV.VI.

65 See Clement, *Miscellanies*, I.XIII.

such. Such a view clearly puts God outside of the normal "before" and "after" sequence of history as we know it. God transcends both time and space, according to Clement: "The First Cause is not then in space, but above both space, and time, and name, and conception."[66]

Of course, an immutable God, who has no qualities, no emotions, no future that is not already present, seems far removed from our everyday knowledge and experience. Clement agreed with Plato that this sort of God cannot be expressed in human language: "For He can by no means be expressed. Well done, Plato! Thou hast touched on the truth."[67] God is invisible to us not only physically, but also rationally and intellectually. Just as we cannot see him with our physical eyes, so too we cannot know or grasp him with our intellects. God is hidden from us, "a Being difficult to grasp and apprehend, ever receding and withdrawing from him who pursues."[68] Clement agreed with Plato that ultimate reality is beyond all human knowledge and predication. He wrote that, according to Plato, it is:

> "a difficult task to discover the Father and Maker of this universe; and having found Him, it is impossible to declare Him to all. For this is by no means capable of expression, like the other subjects of instruction," says the truth-loving Plato. For he that had heard right well that the all-wise Moses, ascending the mount for holy contemplation, to the summit of intellectual objects, necessarily commands that the whole people do not accompany him. And when the Scripture says, "Moses entered into the thick darkness where God was," this shows to those capable of understanding, that God is invisible and beyond expression by words.[69]

---

66 Clement, *Miscellanies*, V.XI.

67 Clement, *Exhortation*, VI.

68 Clement, *Miscellanies*, II.II.

69 Clement, *Miscellanies*, V.XII.

Moses ascended Mount Sinai, apparently, in order to use the Platonic method of intellectual ascent to commune with God. According to Clement, Moses concluded (much like Plato would later) that God cannot ultimately be relayed in words. Likewise, God was unable to show Moses his glory or true self (e.g., in Exodus 33) because "God is not to be known by human wisdom."[70] Clement concluded that Moses and Plato agreed that God is, in the last analysis, unknowable and unknown. Seemingly, this would make Christian theology impossible to the extent that theology purports to teach a knowledge of God; the theologian is, as it were, chained in the cave:

> For the Divine Being cannot be declared as it exists: but as we who are fettered in the flesh were able to listen, so the prophets spake to us; the Lord savingly accommodating Himself to the weakness of men.[71]

According to Clement, though God sometimes presents himself as temporal and mutable in Scripture, he does so out of an accommodating kindness. As a philosopher might address a child in childlike terms rather than in the technical language of philosophy, so too God stoops to man's level to present himself in terms that we can understand and personally relate to. The Bible is true, of course, but cannot reveal God to us as he is, in himself, for we are not divine beings. We are only men, born just moments ago, toiling away our few days in ignorance.

Likewise, for Clement, God, as God, is time-less but nevertheless presents himself in the Bible *as if* he operates in time. God, as God, is simple, but God in the Bible presents himself as manifold and complex. God, as God, is immutable, but the Bible presents God as if he is responsive to external stimuli. God, as God, is impassible, but God in the Bible is presented as experiencing emotion. God *as revealed*

70 Clement, *Miscellanies*, II.II.

71 Clement, *Miscellanies*, II.XVI.

looks much like a man, where God *as he actually is* is quite unlike us. Clement's view is that God, in Scripture, accommodates himself to our weaknesses, yet we are also able to move beyond the child-like language of Scripture to see that God is, in fact, simple, time-less, impassible, and absolutely immutable.

Clement conceded that this sort of being seems far removed from us. In Clement's quote immediately above, the reader will note that God became an impersonal "it" rather than a personal "he," as in Scripture. This is typical of Platonic and Neoplatonic thought, as will be seen more clearly in the chapters to follow. Clement has transformed the personal, relational God of the Bible into an impersonal, non-relational "it."

Clement agreed with Plato that man cannot know God *as God,* because God is strictly unknown to us. Even God himself cannot reveal himself, as himself, in human writing or in human speech:

> For the God of the universe, who is above all speech, all conception, all thought, can never be committed to writing, being inexpressible even by His own power. And this too Plato showed, by saying: "Considering, then, these things, take care lest some time or other you repent on account of the present things, departing in a manner unworthy. The greatest safeguard is not to write, but learn; for it is utterly impossible that what is written will not vanish."[72]

For Clement, given that God, as he really is, cannot express himself in writing, it follows that the God we have in the Bible is not the revelation of God, *as God,* but of God couched in the manner of

---

72 Clement, *Miscellanies,* V.X. It is common sentiment among ancient Platonists to denigrate the act of writing, for all writings are material objects that are doomed to perish in the flux of the material world. Notes get lost, paper decays with time. It is better to think than to write, for, in light of your perennial reincarnation, thinking will stay with you much longer.

our comprehension. We will see this assertion become more explicit—and more problematic—with time.

Clement insisted that our knowledge of God can only be in negative terms. We cannot know what God is, but only what he is not.[73] Clement was one of the earliest Christians to teach what is called apophatic theology, where "apophatic" refers to the Greek term *apophasis* (⊠π⊠⊠⊠⊠⊠), which means "to deny." This type of theologizing borrowed heavily from Neoplatonic sources, and was called the *via negativa* or "negative way" throughout the Middle Ages.[74] Clement seemed to be comfortable identifying Plato's "Good" with the God of the Bible. He also asserted that whatever we positively affirm of God is affirmed only in an improper manner:

> For on account of His greatness He is ranked as the All, and is the Father of the universe. Nor are any parts to be predicated of Him. For the One is indivisible; wherefore also it is infinite...without form and name. And if we name it, we do not do so properly, terming it either the One, or the Good, or Mind, or Absolute Being, or Father, or God, or Creator, or Lord. We speak not as supplying His name; but for want, we use good names...so as not to err in other directions.[75]

Clement assumed that when Paul spoke to the Athenians about the UNKNOWN GOD, that he agreed with them that God is, in the last analysis, unknown to us.[76] Of course, this premise seems quite contrary to Paul's evangelistic endeavors. It hardly seems right to say that Paul believed that pagan thought was already more or less on the right track on the subject of God. Evangelism becomes needless in a scheme where pagan philosophy works just as well.

---

73 Clement, Miscellanies, V.XI.

74 See Copleston, *History*, V2, 26.

75 Clement, *Miscellanies*, V.XII.

76 Clement, *Miscellanies*, V.XII.

Clement was a Platonist through and through. The structure of his worldview is Platonic. It may be illustrated like this:

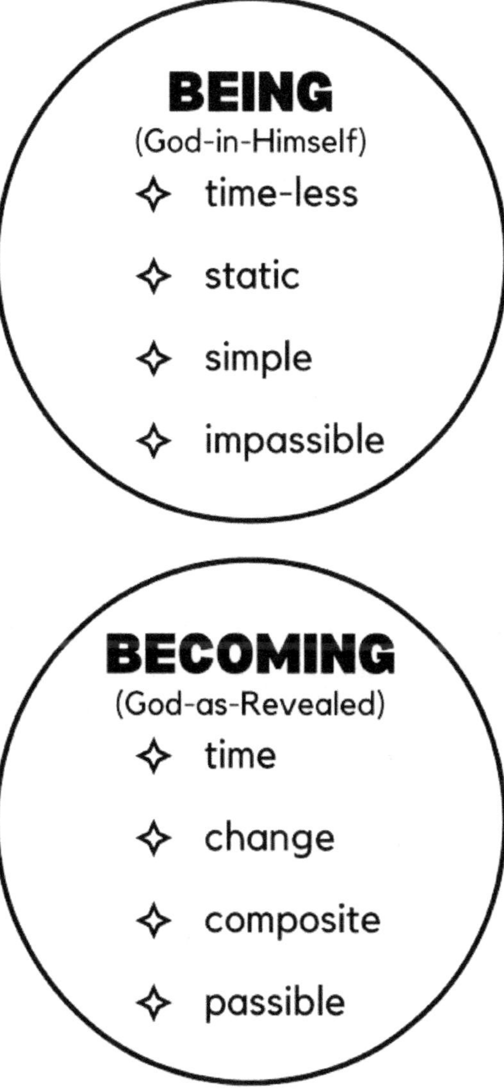

Figure 3: Clement's Platonism

Clement fully embraced the Platonic Divorce. God and man have been *defined* as opposite and as antithetical. Since they are opposites, they stand in both ontic and epistemic isolation from one another. The

God revealed to us in the childlike language of Scripture is quite different, and even quite contrary, to the God that exists as God. Sadly, the God that exists as God is wholly unknown to us.

Based largely on a mistranslation of Isaiah 7:9 in the LXX, Clement said that God must be believed before he could be understood. This ancient adage—repeated by Augustine and others—derived from the Platonic conviction that God, considered in himself, could not properly be revealed in terms of human logic or language. God-in-himself is beyond human predication. God-in-himself is not rational as man knows rationality, and, therefore, we cannot reason our way to God-in-himself. Therefore, faith must come before knowledge. Clement thus established a faith vs. reason dichotomy that would be repeated (most famously, perhaps, in Søren Kierkegaard's "leap of faith") through the present day.

I believe this is a false dichotomy arising from the acceptance of faulty Platonic and Neoplatonic doctrines. Where God is defined in the manner of classical theism, God must forever stand in contrast to human rationality, and faith in such a being must forever stand in contrast to reason. To rid ourselves of the doctrines of classical theism is to simultaneously affirm that faith and reason are complementary rather than competing.

Let me speak frankly, as the simpleton that I am. From a practical perspective, it seems quite disheartening to learn that the God depicted in the Bible is not really the God that actually exists as God. If I believed such a thing (I do not), I think it would discourage me from reading my Bible. For why would I search for God in Scripture if I held as a fundamental belief that God, as God, cannot actually be found there? Clement's view is that the philosopher should seek to *transcend* the God revealed in Scripture, yet the God so discovered is, sadly, UNKNOWN to us.

Admittedly, I have here given a very critical account of Clement's thought. This was necessary for our present purposes, but it should be said that a separate account of his strengths would be needed to get the full picture of his life and thought. Clement was the first Christian theologian to teach the commendable doctrine of creation *ex nihilo*.[77] He anticipated Augustine's view of evil by saying that evil is an action, and not a thing, and, therefore, God could not have created evil. Actions, after all, can't be *created*, they can only be *committed* subsequent to creation. Clement wrote countless pages on the inconsistencies of pagan polytheism, the wickedness of the gods of the poets, and the superficiality of contemporary allegorical interpretations of those same poets.

Clement presented Christianity in philosophical terms that educated pagans could sympathize with, which made him an important apologist in an age of intense persecution. If I fault him for his errors, I will also remind myself that he helped purchase the freedom that made the present rebuttal possible. Little is known about the end of Clement's life; he fled Alexandria amid the persecutions of the Roman Emperor, Septimius Severus (145–211 AD), and died in an unknown location in an unknown year.

77 See Pelikan, *Christian Tradition*, 36.

5

PLOTINUS

PLATO'S successors sought to alleviate the tensions that Plato had so forcefully noted; they could hardly do otherwise. Plato's robust arguments against himself would not allow his doctrines to be accepted without qualifications and amendments.

Scholars today distinguish various phases of Platonism in its historical development, typically labelling the whole movement "Neoplatonism." The name is suitable given genuine differences between Plato's views and those of his successors. It must be kept in mind, however, that this distinction is a very modern distinction. In the ancient world, little distinction was made between the views of Plato's followers and those of Plato himself.

Even in cases of real differences, his followers generally argued they were staying true to their founder. Such was the spirit of the age. A false sense of unity was valued more highly than sharp lines of demarcation. Christians and non-Christians alike treated "Platonism" as a single school with a single, self-consistent body of doctrine. It is thus common to find ancient thinkers attributing views to Plato which Plato himself never held.

Plotinus (c. 204–270 AD) represents the high water mark of Neoplatonic thought. He probed the doctrines of time-lessness and simplicity more than any thinker before him and perhaps even more than any thinker ever since. Little is known of his life. He is said to have taken up the study of philosophy at the age of twenty-eight and to have traveled the world in search of insightful teachers. He began taking on students and lecturing on philosophy in Rome at the age of forty.

Plotinus was a younger contemporary of Clement. Christianity, by this time, was a widespread movement. Curiously, Plotinus never mentions it. We can only speculate as to whether his silence was born of bitterness at Christianity's rapid growth or perhaps the faulty conviction that the movement was merely a passing fancy, quickly to be stamped out by the Roman authorities.

Plotinus' historical significance cannot be overstated. The "Platonism" that dominated the outlook of the Middle Ages was not that of Plato himself, but rather that of Plotinus and his leading student, Porphyry (c. 234–c. 305 AD). Augustine, for example, did not have access to Plato's writings; rather, he learned "Platonism" primarily through Plotinus and Porphyry. According to Inge, "In East and West alike the influence of Plotinus on Catholic dogma, and on the whole intellectual life of the Church, has been enormous, and is still operative."[1]

Plotinus wrote a large number of treatises which were each said to have been written in a single sitting and never subsequently edited by the author, though the story is probably fanciful. The treatises are said to have been divided by his students into six books, each consisting of nine chapters. They were called the "Anneads," a word that refers to a group of nine. The division of the work seems rather arbitrary. It is a very lengthy and challenging work, heavily laden with highly abstract questions. The realist underpinnings of many questions makes them seem nonsensical from a modern, nominalistic perspective.

---

1 Inge, *Plotinus*, V1, 70.

In the writings of Plato, concepts such as the Good, the Demiurge, the Forms, etc., all strike us as independent hypotheses with limited connective tissue. Questions abound but answers are few. When his questions became too taxing and logic seemed to falter, Plato often trailed into mythology to offer a traditional (albeit superficial) answer. We do not really discover a comprehensive "system" of thought in Plato's writings.

Plotinus, on the other hand, is found near the end of a long line of thinkers who turned these independent theories into a comprehensive, systematic belief system. From the modern, Cartesian perspective that philosophy should begin with the least possible number of assumptions and let plain reason lead where it will, the system of Plotinus looks much more like a religion than a philosophy.

For Plotinus, reality consists of three tiers or layers or "hypostases": the Good, Mind, and Soul. He borrowed from Stoicism (and perhaps even from the Christian doctrines of generation and procession) when he argued that each tier of reality emanates out of the previous tier. The Good begets Mind which in turn begets Soul:

> We need not, then, go seeking any other Principles: this—
> the One and the Good—is our First; next to it follows
> the Intellectual Principle [Mind], the Primal Thinker;
> and upon this follows Soul. Such is the order in nature.
> The Intellectual Realm allows no more than these and
> no fewer.[2]

All existence emanates outward and downward from a central hub. Among Plotinus' favorite metaphors, we find that of the sun producing light or a mirror producing a reflection. Plotinus' system can be illustrated as follows:

---

2 Plotinus, *Anneads*, 2.9.1.

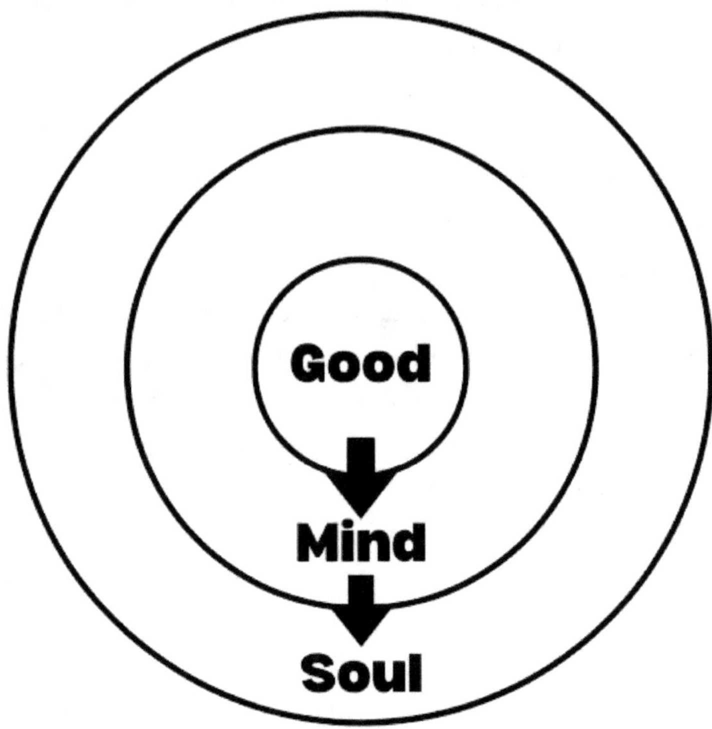

Figure 4: Plotinus' Three Hypostases

Plotinus called this procession "the downward way" inasmuch as the Good was imagined to be higher on the hierarchy of being than Mind, which is higher, in turn, than Soul. Each of the three tiers is further subdivided into two halves, an upper and lower. This process of emanation is a natural and necessary process. For Plotinus, this world is not a product of God's will or arbitrary fiat, but the natural overflow of God's own being:

> The world, we must reflect, is a product of Necessity, not of deliberate purpose: it is due to a higher Kind engendering in its own likeness by a natural process.[3]

3 Plotinus, *Anneads*, 3.2.3.

Inasmuch as all that exists is generated naturally and automatically out of the Good, Plotinus is rightly called a pantheist.[4] In an important sense, all that exists is the Good: "The universe is one living organism."[5] The Good has begotten Mind eternally which has begotten Soul eternally and will continue forever to do so: "We hold that the ordered universe, in its material mass, has existed for ever and will for ever endure."[6] Though all of reality is united as one single organism, the real distinctions within this organism are viewed as fixed and permanent. Perhaps in the way that any individual man is a complex of many distinct organs, so too this world has always existed as a product of the Good in these same three tiers or layers.

The highest reality, the Good, is the source of all other existence, untouchable in its utter transcendence:

> The Good is that on which all else depends, towards which all Existences aspire as to their source and their need, while Itself is without need, sufficient to Itself, aspiring to no other, the measure and Term of all, giving out from itself the Intellectual-Principle [Mind] and Existence and Soul and Life and all Intellective-Act.
>
> All until The Good is reached is beautiful; The Good is beyond beautiful, beyond the Highest, holding kingly state in the Intellectual Kosmos, that sphere constituted by a Principle wholly unlike what is known as Intelligence in us.[7]

Plotinus' conception of the Good seemed to be impersonal, though he commonly referred to the Good as "God", the two terms being used synonymously. In the exposition to follow, I will use the terms "the Good" and "God" interchangeably, just as Plotinus did.

---

4 Or, perhaps, panentheist.

5 Plotinus, *Anneads*, 3.2.7.

6 Plotinus, *Anneads*, 2.1.1.

7 Plotinus, *Anneads*, 1.8.2.

The Good is characterized by its perfect self-unity and utter "partlessness."[8] In other words, God is simple and indivisible, transcendent above all forms of division. Plotinus drew a number of interesting conclusions from his doctrine of simplicity. For one, he claimed that God does not have *knowledge*, properly speaking, for knowledge supposes distinctions between this and that, the differentiation of one object of knowledge from other objects of knowledge. The Good, in its utter simplicity, knows nothing of division.[9] The Good is, therefore, transcendent above knowledge: "All thinking and knowing must here be eliminated: the addition introduces deprivation and deficiency."[10] For Plotinus, attributing knowledge to God would be attributing a limitation to God. God is transcendent above knowledge.

Again, we are immediately confronted with the Platonic Divorce between two modes of reality which could never know one another. Knowledge, as we know it, presupposes multiplicity. If God has no multiplicity, neither can he have a knowledge of multiple, diverse things. Plotinus reasoned that since God is simple and has no internal distinctions, neither can he be aware of any external distinctions. An awareness of distinctions external to himself would suppose familiarity with distinctions, but a simple being cannot have such an awareness. An awareness of external distinctions, in other words, would presuppose a measure of internal distinction inasmuch as that which is known is distinct and "other" than God himself. For Plotinus, the Good has no distinctions and knows no distinctions. Therefore, the Good has no knowledge.

This seems to raise an interesting question for Christians who advocate the doctrine of divine simplicity: is God's knowledge of me identical to God? Since advocates of simplicity argue that whatever is in God is identical to God, I think they would have to concede that

---

8 Plotinus, *Anneads*, 3.7.6.

9 Plotinus, *Anneads*, 3.7.6.

10 Plotinus, *Anneads*, 3.9.3.

the answer is yes. From here it is but a small step to say that since God's knowledge of God is identical to God, and since God's knowledge of me is identical to God, then it follows that God and I are identical. Plotinus' pantheism, from this perspective, seems a logical consequence of his thorough-going doctrine of simplicity.

According to Plotinus, the Good does not even know itself, for self-consciousness entails a distinction between subject and object. When thinking about my own plans for tomorrow, for instance, the self that I imagine in an imaginary tomorrow is not exactly identical to the self that actually exists in the present. Self-consciousness entails a distinction between the self as a thinking subject and the self as an object of thought. Since God is simple and knows no distinctions, God, therefore, cannot be self-conscious.

Plotinus, like Plato, argued that we cannot ultimately predicate anything of the Good:

> Once you have uttered "The Good," add no further thought: by any addition, and in proportion to that addition, you introduce a deficiency. Do not even say that it has Intellection; you would be dividing it; it would become a duality, Intellect and the Good.[11]

Whatever we attribute to the Good is attributed improperly. Even to say that the Good "exists" is not true, strictly speaking, for the Good is *beyond* being and existence.[12] Though we aspire to know God, our aspirations are, strictly speaking, "not correct."[13] Even to say that the Good *is good* is not strictly true; rather, the simple Good is identical with its goodness in a manner that is unknowable to us. The Good is far too transcendent to be limited by the human notion of "goodness":

---

11 Plotinus, *Anneads*, 3.8.10.

12 See Plotinus, *Anneads*, 1.7.1.

13 Fitzgerald, ed., *Augustine*, 654, (6.8.13).

> And yet this "He Is" does not truly apply: the Supreme has no need of Being: even "He is good" does not apply since it indicates Being: the "is" should not suggest something predicated of another thing; it is to state identity. The word "good" used of him is not a predicate asserting his possession of goodness; it conveys an identification. It is not that we think it exact to call him either good or The Good: it is that sheer negation does not indicate; we use the term The Good to assert identity without the affirmation of Being.
>
> But how admit a Principle void of self-knowledge, self-awareness; surely the First must be able to say "I possess Being?"
>
> But he does not possess Being.
>
> Then, at least he must say "I am good?"
>
> No: once more, that would be an affirmation of Being.[14]

The Good is beyond "being" as we understand being. Our human categories simply don't apply, because there is no epistemological common ground between us and it, no similarities whatsoever. Nothing can properly be predicated of it; nothing properly attributed to it. Of the Good we can say nothing.[15] Language fails us, since it cannot convey anything of the Good.[16] Nothing can positively be ascribed to God:

> Thus we rob it of its very being as The Absolute Good if we ascribe anything to it, existence or intellect or goodness. The only way is to make every denial and no assertion, to feign

14 Plotinus, *Anneads*, 6.7.38.

15 See Inge, *Plotinus*, V2, 75. See Plotinus, *Anneads*, 6.2.17.

16 Plotinus, *Anneads*, 6.8.13.

> no quality or content there but to permit only the "It is" in which we pretend to no affirmation...[17]

According to Plotinus, "We can and do state what it is *not*, while we are silent as to what it *is*."[18] I'm not at all convinced that this apophatic, Neoplatonic line of reasoning is coherent. When I say what something is *not*, I have simultaneously carved out a definite, defining boundary line regarding that of which I speak. If I say my house is *not* yellow, I have simultaneously limited the range of possibilities about what color my house might be. Every negation implies some positive affirmation, however vague. To be consistent, Plotinus should say neither *what God is* nor *what God is not*. Since nothing can be affirmed of God—the Good—one way or the other, it would seemingly be more consistent for Plotinus to stop speaking altogether. It is quite vain and self-defeating, after all, to attempt to define the indefinable or apply words to that to which words cannot apply. Plotinus nevertheless continued on for countless pages.

The Good has no needs; it aspires to nothing. It neither strives for anything nor attains anything.[19] It does not move or *act*, because action supposes change, and the Good is absolutely unchanging or immutable. Accordingly, we must deny that God knows anything of time, for time is change and succession and division, where God is simple, without division. Each moment past is now extinct; God knows nothing of extinction and therefore nothing of time.[20] The Good is "outside" of time:

> Now the life of the Authentic-Existence [Good] is measurable not by time but by eternity; and eternity is not a more or a less or a thing of any magnitude but is the unchangeable, the indivisible, is timeless Being.

17 Plotinus, *Anneads*, 5.5.13.

18 Plotinus, *Anneads*, 5.2.14.

19 Plotinus, *Anneads*, 3.8.10.

20 Plotinus, *Anneads*, 1.5.7.

> We must not muddle together Being and Non-Being, time and eternity, not even everlasting time with the eternal; we cannot make laps and stages of an absolute unity; all must be taken together, wheresoever and howsoever we handle it; and it must be taken at that, not even as an undivided block of time but as the Life of Eternity, a stretch not made up of periods but completely rounded, outside of all notion of time.[21]

Plotinus defined eternity as a state in which the past and the future are all equally present to God. God has no past and no future, as such: "Nowhere is there any future, for every then is a now; nor is there any past, for nothing there has ever ceased to be; everything has taken its stand for ever, an identity well pleased, we might say, to be as it is."[22]

Time supposes distinctions of past, present, and future, but God knows no distinctions and thus exists as if at a single point "instantaneously entire."[23] If God had a history, part of which was past, then God would be composed of parts.[24] A simple God cannot have a history, for he has no life that can be divided up into segments. Simplicity thus seems to presuppose time-lessness, for time-lessness is imaged to be a sort of indivisible and immutable time. Though man is distinct from his surrounding environment, the simple God cannot be distinct from his own situation. God is thus identical to his own eternity.[25]

Likewise, God should not be thought of as extended in space, nor as existing in any particular location. "There is an instantaneous presence everywhere, nothing containing and nothing left void…"[26] It is "spaceless;"[27] time and space are strictly inapplicable to God.

---

21 Plotinus, *Anneads*, 1.5.73.

22 Plotinus, *Anneads*, 5.1.4.

23 Plotinus, *Anneads*, 3.7.3.

24 See Plotinus, *Anneads*, 3.7.3.

25 Plotinus, *Anneads*, 3.7.5.

26 Plotinus, *Anneads*, 5.5.10.

27 Plotinus, *Anneads*, 6.8.11.

According to Plotinus, God has no memory, for memory supposes distinctions of time and place, but the simple God has no involvement with distinctions. Likewise, memory supposes a recollection of things past, but the Good has no past, as such. The Good, therefore, as time-less and space-less, possesses no memory.[28]

The Good produces a second: Mind. The production of Mind out of the Good is a natural emanation, like a mirror reflecting the image of a face.[29] It is not a willful creation but a natural, necessary overflow:

> Seeking nothing, possessing nothing, lacking nothing, the One is perfect and, in our metaphor, has overflowed, and its exuberance has produced the new: this product has turned again to its begetter and been filled and has become its contemplator and so an Intellectual-Principle [Mind].[30]

Mind is the reflection or image of the Good. Mind is likened to the mind of God.[31] Mind tries, as far as it is able, to (metaphorically) imitate its father.[32] Yet the reflection, as a reflection, is not strictly identical to the original. Mind is the first appearance of multiplicity and of self-consciousness. Mind is the very first life (since the Good is beyond life).[33] Mind is also the beginning of multiplicity and of thought and self-consciousness. Mind is likened to Plato's Demiurge.[34] Mind is the storehouse of the unchanging Forms.

Mind generates a third layer of reality: Soul. As Mind is a copy of the Good, so too is Soul a copy of Mind. Just as our words reflect

28 Plotinus, *Anneads*, 4.2.24.

29 Plotinus, *Anneads*, 1.1.8.

30 Plotinus, *Anneads*, 5.2.1.

31 See Plotinus, *Anneads*, 5.1.6.

32 Plotinus, *Anneads*, 2.9.2.

33 Plotinus, *Anneads*, 3.8.9.

34 Plotinus, *Anneads*, 5.1.10.

our internal thoughts, so too Soul reflects Mind.[35] Soul is the beginning of motion.[36] It is not until we arrive at Soul, the lowest tier of reality, that we find time.[37] Soul was envisioned as a world-soul that gives life and breath and motion to all creatures, including the stars and planetary bodies.

Soul is divided into two parts, an upper and lower. In its upper half it is simple and indivisible, like the Good. Since it is indivisible, we know that the entirety of Soul dwells in every living creature.[38] Soul gives unity to our diverse sensations and imparts to us some measure of unchanging knowledge, as found in Mind. Soul gives us a measure of empathy with one another since we all share the "self-same soul."[39] This helps to explain why all men have similar conceptions of love, beauty, square roots, infinity, and the like. Though we all share a single soul, the exact condition of this unity is obscured by matter.

In its lower half, Soul is composite and divisible. At this lowest stage of reality, it generates matter. Matter is unthinking but bears the marks of intelligent patterns; thus we see the intelligent influence of Mind upon matter.[40] Plotinus' conception of matter is quite curious. At times, he sounds like a cosmological dualist who envisions a never-ending battle between evil matter and the immaterial "Good." On the whole, however, he sees matter not as a real evil, but simply as an unreal illusion. Matter is not described as a fourth tier of reality; rather, it is an illusory un-reality. Matter is not being but non-being, the most distant echo or termination point of the Good's (finite) overflow. The reflection of the Good in matter is so distant and distorted that it is difficult to recognize the Good in it at all. Matter and man's bad deeds

35 Plotinus, *Anneads*, 5.1.3.

36 Plotinus, *Anneads*, 5.2.1.

37 Plotinus, *Anneads*, 3.7.11.

38 Plotinus, *Anneads*, 4.2.1.

39 Plotinus, *Anneads*, 4.2.8.

40 Plotinus, *Anneads*, 4.7.3.

are nearly one and the same. "Thus the cause, at once, of the weakness of Soul and of all its evil is Matter."[41] Evil and matter are sometimes said to be one and the same.[42] In accordance with his view that matter is non-being, practically identical to evil, Plotinus' students said he appeared uncomfortable and ashamed to stand before them in a physical body. (Plotinus accounted the gift of a physical body to be a curse. All non-Christian philosophy is practically constricting in one way or another, since it always misapprehends the facts of our situation).[43]

Plotinus defined human morality as the imitation of Mind (itself an imitation of the Good), and, like Plato, suggested that moral behavior leads to a higher state of being in subsequent lives in the perpetual cycle of transmigration. Yet the necessity of evil in Plotinus' system, as a permanent fixture of reality, makes this appeal seem quite shallow. A man may become a snail if he is bad and a king if he is good, but in any case, given an infinite amount of time, he will eventually be both a snail and a king over and over again. The cycle of perpetual change dominates all of this lower reality and we can never attain a higher state of being. Thus, moral effort seems of little lasting consequence. Plotinus was ultimately forced to acknowledge that evil is good inasmuch as evil, like everything else, is a product of the Good. What we call evil is mostly just ignorance of the Good in everything. Like everything else, evil is born of necessity.[44]

Plotinus agreed with Plato that man must disregard his physicality and foster the abilities of his soul and especially of his mind. This is the "upward way" by which the philosopher traces the chain of being back up the hierarchical ladder to its original source in the Good. Where reality emanates downward, philosophy draws man upward into the contemplation of the higher modes of reality. As in

41 Plotinus, *Anneads*, 1.8.11.

42 See Plotinus, *Anneads*, 3.6.11.

43 Which I learned from Francis Schaeffer and Os Guinness.

44 Plotinus, *Anneads*, 3.3.5.

Plato, man's chief end lies in intellectual contemplation. Man becomes more like the Good as he moves away from physical sensuality toward a disconnected contemplation of static notions. Plotinus did not seem to place much value upon personal immortality; the philosopher, lost in abstract thought, becomes more like the divine as personal memories are forgotten and personal identity is lost.[45]

William Inge offers this eloquent summary of the philosophy of Plotinus:

> The universe is a living chain of Being, a 'harmony' in the Greek sense of the word. The divine life overflows in an incessant stream of creative activity, so that every possible manifestation of divine energy, in degree as well as in kind, is somewhere represented. There is a corresponding centripetal movement of all created things back to the divine: such is the systole and diastole of universal life.[46]

On occasion, Plotinus spoke of a mystical vision by which we can leave the realm below and achieve a momentary identity with the Good.[47] Plotinus said he had these experiences several times. In recounting these experiences, he told us that he found the Good to be quite noble and beautiful. Of course, such an account is inconsistent with his premise that nothing can be predicated of the Good. If nothing can positively be said of the Good, then Plotinus' positive accounts of the experience are most definitely suspect.

Plotinus did not seem to fully appreciate that it is inconsistent to say that nothing can be predicated of God and yet say that such a being as God "exists." To posit the existence of such a thing as God is to say that you know something about what it is that you're asserting the existence of. Obviously, it is self-defeating to posit an unknown thing that

45 Plotinus, *Anneads*, 4.2.31.

46 Inge, *Plotinus*, V1, xix.

47 See Plotinus, *Anneads*, 4.8.1.

you *know* about. If the human notion of "existence" is strictly inapplicable to the Good, as Plotinus insisted, then it is no more meaningful to say that the Good *exists* than it is to say that the Good *doesn't exist.* If "existence" is inapplicable, then neither premise is more meaningful or defensible than the other.

I cannot help but wonder, since Plotinus denied that our knowledge of the Good has any positive content, why does he not call it *the Bad* instead of the Good? It seems we would do well to return to Socrates and ask what knowledge of this absolutely UNKNOWN can we hope to glean from reading Plotinus? Plotinus left us with an absurd mysticism in which we must struggle to imagine that which is necessarily unimaginable. He imagines this struggle to be a matter of humility, but we need to be clear that this is a false humility. Let's be frank. If God is unknowable, then let's be consistent and stop trying to know him. If God is literally unspeakable, then let us speak of him no longer. You cannot *know* an unknowable God. Nor could you know that there is such a being.

There is a clear tendency in Neoplatonism to try to soften the force of the Platonic Divorce by adding intermediary stages between the two antithetical modes of being. Seemingly, these intermediary phases help to ease the inherent tension in Platonism between the manifold and the simple, time and the time-less, the mutable and the immutable, the knowable and the unknown. Ultimately, however, the tension remains. Plotinus used the lowest tier—the Soul tier—to make the transition from time-less simplicity to the manifold world of time, but the transition still strikes us as abrupt, leaving Plotinus with precisely the same epistemological problem as Plato:

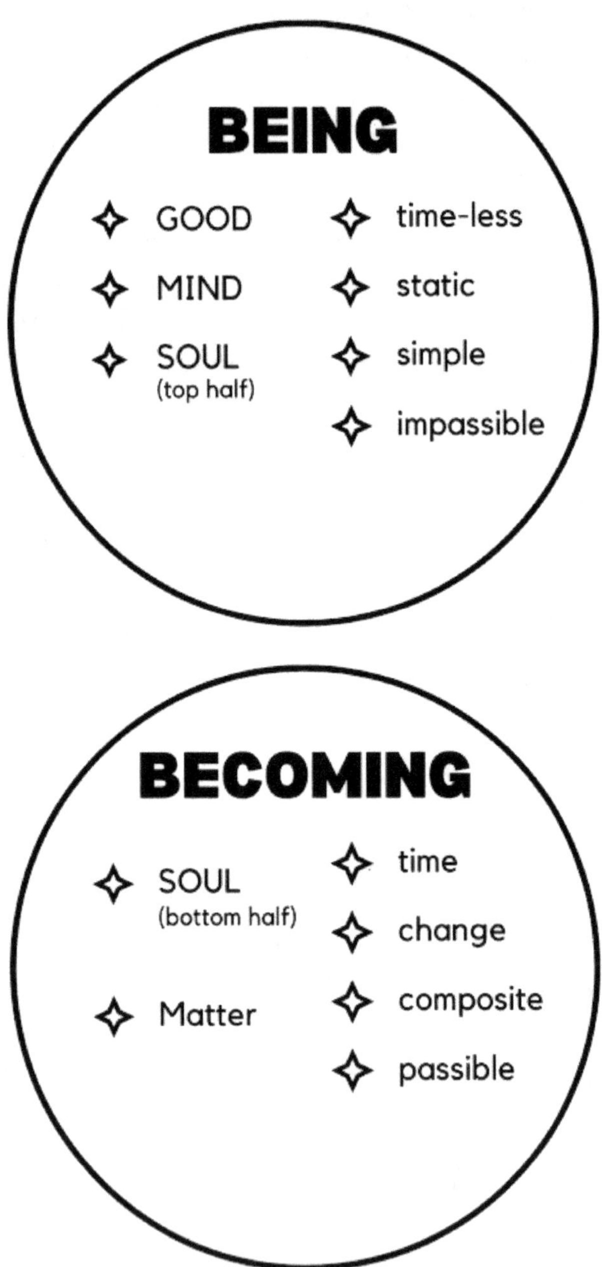

Figure 5: Plotinus' Platonism

Like Plato, Plotinus asserted that there is a simple and time-less mode of existence. To a greater extent than Plato, he carried this to its logical conclusion. Since man is neither simple nor time-less, it follows that man cannot not have any knowledge of this contrary, antithetical mode of being. Man cannot know God because man's mode of being is the practical opposite of God's mode of being. There cannot be any epistemological middle ground between time-lessness and time. There cannot be any epistemological middle ground between the simple and manifold. Plotinus' search for the UNKNOWN GOD must, therefore, be accounted a failure. All subsequent attempts to attain a knowledge of the unknowable were likewise foredoomed.

6

AUGUSTINE

AUGUSTINE (354–430 AD) is a towering figure in Christian theology, and for good reason. He had a powerful mind and approached difficult questions soberly, systematically, and always with a spirit of humble reliance upon God. At every turn, Augustine demonstrated intense and penetrating insight. His combination of brilliance and modesty makes him attractive to most every intelligent reader, Christian or not. No other extra-biblical author has a greater claim to being the architect of Christian orthodoxy. Augustine sketched the boundary lines within which most later discussions would be held.

I can only lament that the design of the present work will not allow us to examine Augustine's work as a whole. He was, undoubtedly, a masterful theologian and philosopher. Unfortunately, this is more a history of blemishes than of successes. Our main concerns here will be with the influence of Platonism upon Augustine's thought and his exposition of the doctrines of immutability, time-lessness, simplicity, and impassibility.

Augustine described the intellectual journey that led to his conversion to Christianity in his famous work, *Confessions*. We will, for the most part, follow the path he laid out for us there. He was born in the Roman province of Numidia, on the North African coast. His father was a pagan and his mother a devoted Christian. Augustine felt little sympathy for his mother's outlook early on; his father exerted the greater influence. At age nineteen, he took the advice of the famous Roman author, Cicero (106–43 BC), to pursue the study of philosophy.[1] Prior to this, he was focused on becoming a persuasive speaker in hopes of garnering human applause. Henceforth, he became an avid student of philosophy, with a fundamental interest in discovering the true system of thought through rational means. In *Confessions*, he described a lengthy process of what we might call worldview elimination. The various philosophies of the day all seemed to have internal inconsistencies, leading Augustine to reject one philosophy after another as he searched for the one, true belief system.

Throughout his twenties, Augustine was a materialist. He believed that only material objects exist and that God and evil were both material entities. He imagined that the material God was locked in a perpetual, unresolved conflict with the material evil.[2] For a time he fell in with the Manichean philosophers who likewise taught that good and evil are trapped in a dualistic, material conflict.

Augustine said he had trouble imagining invisible, spiritual beings. As with many folks in our own day, Augustine automatically deemed everything non-material as non-existent. This proved to be a great hindrance to his acceptance of the Christian message, which, of course, described God as an invisible, spiritual being. His initial contact with Platonism proved an important stepping stone in this regard. As is familiar by now, the Platonists argued that the physical world is deficient and misleading as a source of knowledge and that we should gaze upon the invisible and immaterial. Similarly, Plato had described the immaterial soul in sharp contrast to the physical body. This contact opened Augustine's eyes to the possibility of the existence

1 Augustine, *Confessions*, 3.4 (18).

2 See Augustine, *Confessions*, 5.10 (41).

of non-material entities. Augustine's presentation of his first encounter with Platonism is quite curious:

> So you [God] made use of a man, one who was bloated with the most outrageous pride, to procure me some of the books of the Platonists, translated from the Greek into Latin. In them I read—not, of course, word for word, though the sense was the same and it was supported by all kinds of different arguments—that at the beginning of time the Word already was; and God had the Word abiding with him, and the Word was God. He abode, at the beginning of time, with God. It was through him that all things came into being, and without him came nothing that has come to be.[3]

Augustine continued to quote John's gospel for several paragraphs. His point was not that the Platonists actually quoted John the Apostle. His point, rather, was that the Platonists were in essential harmony with Scriptural teaching in some areas. The words were different but "the sense was the same." According to Augustine, the Platonists substantially agreed with some elements of Scripture:

> Though the words were different and the meaning was expressed in various ways, I also learned from these books that God the Son, being himself, like the Father, of divine nature, did not see, in the rank of Godhead, a prize to be coveted [Philipians 2:6].[4]

Augustine's rhetorical positioning seems to reflect his belief that when the Platonists wrote about God, they wrote about the true God

3 Augustine, *Confessions*, 7.9 (60).

4 Augustine, *Confessions*, 7.9 (60).

with a substantial degree of accuracy, including even truths about the relationship between God the Father and God the Son.

Augustine didn't tell us which "books of the Platonists" he obtained from his arrogant acquaintance, though he did give us one important clue. He said that they were Latin translations of Greek texts translated by one Victorinus.[5] We know that Victorinus—Gaius Marius Victorinus (290–364 AD)—translated works by Plotinus and his student Porphyry, though these translations have been lost. It is, therefore, nearly certain that the works in question were from the school of Plotinus.

Augustine had very little interaction with the actual writings of Plato. According to one scholar, he "had little firsthand knowledge of Plato. What knowledge he does have is mostly filtered through secondary sources, Cicero's translation of [Plato's] *Timaeus* aside. Middle Platonism, Vergil, Cicero, Varro, Apuleius, Plotinus, Porphyry, and various encyclopedias and doxographies all play a role in passing such knowledge to him."[6] Though explicit references to Plato appear some 252 times in the works of Augustine,[7] the "Plato" that Augustine knew was Plato reinterpreted by the school of Plotinus.

Augustine seems to have thought of Plotinus as the most accurate commentator on Plato and not necessarily as an original thinker in his own right. "Plotinus," he wrote, "whose memory is quite recent, enjoys the reputation of having understood Plato better than any other of his disciples."[8] Since Augustine did not have direct access to the works of Plato, he had little means to question the authority of Plotinus upon the subject.

Shortly after his initial contact with Platonism, Augustine obtained some books of the Bible. Once again, he does not tell us

---

5 Augustine, *Confessions*, 8.2 (67).

6 Fitzgerald, ed., *Augustine*, 653.

7 Fitzgerald, ed., *Augustine*, 651.

8 Augustine, *City of God*, 9.10 (340).

which books, but he tells us that he was happy to discover that they agreed with the Platonists: "I began to read and discovered that whatever truth I had found in the Platonists was set down here as well."[9] Thus, according to Augustine, the truth "found in the Platonists" was discovered to be the same truth "set down" in Scripture. To a great extent, then, Augustine agreed with Clement that the Platonists taught the same system of truth as the Bible, albeit only partially and not with infallible accuracy.

After sitting under the teaching of Ambrose of Milan (339–397 AD) for a time, Augustine's objections to Christianity were assuaged. His mother's tearful prayers were finally answered in 386 AD. Augustine was thirty-one at the time of his conversion. He immediately gave up his (second) mistress as well as a formal betrothal to another woman to live a celibate, monastic life.

Augustine expressed gratitude to God for having stumbled upon the works of the Platonists before he had read Scripture, because if this order had been reversed, "I might have thought it possible for a man who read nothing but the Platonists books to derive the same spirit from them alone."[10] Fortunately, the ordering of his experience helped him to see the necessity of Scripture for personal salvation. The Platonist works, he noted, were missing the important element of the atoning death of Jesus. Though Augustine believed the works of the Platonists were quite often correct, he also believed they were incomplete. Augustine did not go so far as Clement as to account Plato a prophet, or even a true believer. However, he did suggest that many of the Platonists could have been Christians by simply changing a few words here and there.[11]

9 Augustine, *Confessions*, 7.21 (65).

10 Augustine, *Confessions*, 7.20 (65).

11 Augustine, *De vera religione*. Noted in Fitzgerald, *Augustine*, 652.

Augustine seems to have been comfortable identifying the Neoplatonic "Good" with the Christian God.[12] "The Platonic philosophers," he wrote, "have recognized the true God as the author of all things, the source of the light of truth, and the bountiful bestower of all blessedness."[13] Elsewhere, he wrote that at least some of "the Platonists" worship "the one God of gods, who is both theirs and ours."[14] Likewise, he said that Socrates recognized that "the one true and supreme God" was the ultimate cause of all things.[15]

For a time, Augustine accepted the conjecture of Justin Martyr that Plato had traveled to Egypt where he met the Hebrew prophet, Jeremiah, who taught him about God and Scripture.[16] This view originated from Philo and was also endorsed by Clement and Ambrose.[17] Augustine eventually realized that Plato was born at least a century after Jeremiah's death, and could not have met up with him in Egypt.[18]

This again demonstrates how favorably Plato was viewed by the early church fathers. Even the great early church historian, Eusebius of Caesarea (c. 260–c. 339 AD), entertained the notion that Plato was directly influenced by Old Testament prophets. Eusebius went so far as to suggest that Plato, like Moses, was a prophet of salvation.[19]

Like Clement, Augustine accepted the literal existence of Plato's Forms. According to the British historian of philosophy, Anthony Kenny, "Augustine was a Platonist in the straightforward sense that he accepted Plato's theory of ideas or forms."[20] Where Plato described

---

12 See Augustine, *City of God*, 22.26 (689).

13 Augustine, *City of God*, 8.5 (315).

14 Augustine, *City of God*, 10.3 (350).

15 Augustine, *City of God*, 8.3 (313).

16 See Augustine, *On Christian Doctrine*, 2.28 (732). See also, Fitzgerald, ed., *Augustine*, 652.

17 See Copleston, *History*, V2, 15.

18 See Augustine, *City of God*, 319.

19 See Copleston, *History*, V2, 30.

20 Kenny, *God*, 16.

the Forms as external to the Demiurge, Augustine followed those Neoplatonists who placed the Forms inside the mind of God.[21] He noted that Plato was the first to use the term "ideas" in the technical, philosophical sense, though he suggested that other wise men had some grasp of these Forms prior to Plato. In an early work, Augustine described the Forms as follows:

> The ideas are certain original and principal forms of things, i.e., reasons, fixed and unchangeable, which are not themselves formed and, being thus eternal and existing always in the same state, are contained in the Divine Intelligence. And though they themselves neither come into being nor pass away, nevertheless, everything which can come into being and pass away and everything which does come into being and pass away is said to be formed in accord with these ideas.[22]

The doctrine that the time-less Forms were contained within the mind of God enjoyed nearly universal assent in the ancient and medieval church. Copleston noted, "This doctrine was the common doctrine in the Middle Ages up to and including the thirteenth century."[23] It was generally agreed that even though humans imagine a multitude of Forms (the Form of a man, the Form of a bed, the Form of a horse, and so on) the Forms are a simple unity in the mind of the simple God. In other words, though there are many Forms from our perspective, from God's perspective, there is really only one solitary Form. Since God is simple, it was natural to conclude that this one, supreme Form was identical to God himself.

Placing Plato's Forms inside the mind of God still left questions, of course. Are the Forms merely abstract notions in God's mind? Or

---

21 See Fitzgerald, ed., *Augustine*, 652.

22 Augustine, *Questions*, 80.

23 Copleston, *History*, V3, 49.

should we continue to think of them in Platonic terms, as independent objects with a life of their own? If we choose the former option, the Forms become practically useless—just imaginative mental pictures like humans have. In that case, God could undoubtedly change the Forms at his will, and it would be meaningless to describe them as unchanging and eternal. If we pick the latter option, then the Forms would seemingly have some independent, eternal existence beyond God's control, in which case they would seemingly be co-ultimate with God, much as they were for the Demiurge. In either case, placing Plato's Forms in the mind of God seemed problematic.

Though the acceptance of Plato's Forms may seem harmless enough in itself, the acceptance of Plato's time-less, simple, "fixed and unchangeable" Forms implied the acceptance of the Platonic Divorce whereby the time-less, simple, static realm could not bear any real epistemic point of contact with our realm of time and manifold complexity. Practically speaking, God's realm and our realm had been defined as mutually exclusive in such a scheme.

In the context of *Confessions*, God's immutability seems to be a dominant, guiding principle. God is "the Truth which does not change."[24] God stands in sharp contrast with the created order with regard to change: "All of these things are subject to change, but you remain supreme over all things, immutable."[25] According to Augustine, eternity implies strict immutability: "A thing cannot properly be called eternal if it undergoes change in any way."[26] Augustine concluded that God "absolutely cannot change."[27] His view was that God does not change, whereas time is practically identical to change. God is always the same, but "it is the nature of time to change."[28]

24 Augustine, *Confessions*, 11.8 (116).

25 Augustine, *Confessions*, 10.26 (102).

26 Augustine, *Trinity*, 4.4.23 (169).

27 Augustine, *Trinity*, 5.1.3 (190).

28 Augustine, *Confessions*, 3.7 (21).

Since time is always passing away, "we cannot rightly say that time *is*, except by reason of its impending state of *not being*."[29] Time is always *becoming*; it stands always on the verge of non-existence, whereas God is pure, unchanging *being*.

Countless commentators have noted that Augustine's conception of God's relationship to time borrowed heavily from the Neoplatonists.[30] According to Augustine, God created time; time is, therefore, not merely a subjective convention, but an objective (presumably material) creation. God has no past or future, according to Augustine, for all is present at once:

> But in eternity nothing moves into the past: all is present. Time, on the other hand, is never all present at once. The past is always driven on by the future, the future always follows on the heels of the past, and both the past and the future have their beginning and their end in the eternal present. If only men's minds could be seized and held still! They would see how eternity, in which there is neither past nor future, determines both past and future time.[31]

For Augustine, God is imagined to occupy a state of eternal presence. Augustine seems to have overlooked the fact that the notion of the "present" is still a time-referent, however. When we speak of the "present," we are, of course, talking about things that are happening currently, but nothing can "happen" without time. There cannot be thought or action, as we know thought and action, without time. It's not clear what the "present" would be in a situation where nothing new ever transpired. Augustine's notion of an indivisible, perpetual present seemed wrought with difficulties.

---

29 Augustine, *Confessions*, 11.14 (118). Emphasis in original.

30 See Fitzgerald, ed., *Augustine*, 656.

31 Augustine, *Confessions*, 11.11 (117).

Augustine insisted that God's time-less eternity encompasses all ages of time. "The whole series of all times is timelessly contained in God's eternal Wisdom."[32] All human ages consist of a finite duration and, in comparison with God's ever-present eternity, are so small as to be either "the very minutest thing, or nothing at all."[33] Augustine contrasts the human perception of time with the divine perception of time:

> It is not as if the knowledge of God were [of] various kinds, knowing in different ways things which as yet are not, things which are, and things which have been. For not in our fashion does He look forward to what is future, nor at what is present, nor back upon what is past; but in a manner quite different and far and profoundly remote from our way of thinking. For he does not pass from this to that by transition of thought, but beholds all things with absolute unchangeableness; so that of those things which [we see] emerge in time, the future, indeed, are not yet, and the present are now, and the past no longer are; but all these are by Him comprehended in His stable and eternal presence.[34]

For God, the future is always present and thus it is not really the "future" at all. Though many people were vainly inquiring about what God was doing before creation, Augustine noted that it is meaningless to ask about what was happening "before" time, because there is no "before" or "after" in God's time-less eternity:

> It is therefore true to say that when you had not made anything, there was no time, because time itself was of your making. And no time is co-eternal with you, because you never change; whereas if time never changed, it would not be time.[35]

---

32 Augustine, *Trinity*, 2.2.8 (103).

33 Augustine, *City of God*, 12.13 (404).

34 Augustine, *City of God*, 11.21 (386).

35 Augustine, *Confessions*, 11.14 (117-118).

God certainly existed before time, but it must be kept in mind that the "before" is only from man's perspective. From God's perspective, it would not be true to say that God predates his creation, because God has no past or future that is not always uniformly, unchangeably present. A time-less God cannot "pre-date" anything, strictly speaking, for he has no dealings with "dates," as such. If God is time-less, then creation is not a past event for God, for God would have no past, as such. According to Augustine, God is immutable and static; he has no history in the human sense, no sequential timeline.

This seemed to raise several problems regarding the process of creation. If God doesn't change in any sense and, therefore, doesn't *act* or *operate* in the sense that we understand these terms, then what exactly could kick off the creative process in time? Seemingly, a time-less God could not begin to create the world, for "beginning" a process such as creation presupposes time. A time-less God could never *begin* anything in our sense of the word. A time-less, immutable God must always be doing exactly the same thing he has always been doing. So what change could trigger the beginning of creation? Augustine hinted at the Neoplatonic solution that creation is the result of a natural process rather than a conscious decision:

> In the Beginning you knew heaven and earth, and there was no change in your knowledge. In just the same way, in the beginning you created heaven and earth, and there was no change in your action. Some understand this and some do not: let all alike praise you.[36]

God created the world, but no new action on God's part was involved. I confess that I stand among those who don't understand what this means. Augustine's point is plain enough, however: a time-less, immutable God cannot perform new actions. New actions would

36 Augustine, *Confessions*, 11.31 (126).

require God to change, but God does not change. Regarding the Creator, "we cannot say that there has been that which now is not, or shall be that which is not yet."[37] For Augustine, this meant that God is forever doing what he has always been doing in his immutable, eternal present. Our human, temporal understanding of what it means to "create" something is strictly inapplicable to God himself.

Of course, the Bible depicts God as willfully creating the world, step by step, day by day, part by part, successively, in time. According to Genesis, he created one thing after another in a logical, discursive sequence. He couldn't create the birds until he had created the land masses for them to rest upon, and so forth. It is natural to assume that this was the time of his choosing, the time to carry out his plan, purpose, and will. It is natural to assume that his planning and will are distinct within himself, such that he could have postponed creation another few millennia or could have simply decided to call the whole thing off. God is not obligated to create, and creation is certainly not a natural process; yet these very orthodox affirmations seem to suppose that God's will is distinct from his being, and that God is, therefore, not simple. Augustine would not allow such a conception because a time-less God cannot do anything other than what he has always been doing. Nor can he *will* anything other than what he has always been willing. God's essence or being, after all, is identical to his will on account of his simplicity.[38]

To my knowledge, Augustine did not elaborate on his precise meaning as to how God created the world without performing any new actions. It is natural to assume that he agreed with Plotinus that creation was a natural overflow rather than a divine fiat or arbitrary act of will. Though he does not address this particular question, Augustine's many extant writings on the opening pages of Genesis quite clearly

37 Augustine, *City of God*, 12.15 (407).

38 Augustine, *Confessions*, 12.15 (130).

indicate that he preferred an allegorical interpretation of the entire Genesis creation account.

Another difficulty with Augustine's view of God's time-lessness is that a time-less God could not know the facts of time. Or, to speak more strictly, the time-less God could not know the facts of time in a temporal manner. Take the act of creation, for example. For God, the act of creation would still be a present event, though to us it is a past event. In his eternal present (his state of "eternal now" as it is sometimes said), God is presumably still presently creating time, and will always be doing so. Given that God perceives all events as present, God would seemingly be unable to recognize the creation as a past event.

Augustine argued that prayers of the past and prayers of the future are all one to God.[39] God sees all prayers as present, in other words, and does not recognize them as past or future. Yet it hardly seems like a description of omniscience to say that God does not understand time as time. If God does not know temporal facts in the temporal manner, then obviously he does not know all that can be known. Contemporary Christian philosopher, Nicholas Wolterstorff, argues that some facts cannot be stated in time-less terms. He provides the following example:

> That *Calvin's flight from Geneva occurs in 1537* is something that can be known at any and every time whatsoever. For it is both true, and constant in its truth value. But *that Calvin's flight from Geneva is occurring* is variable in its truth value. It once was true, it now is false. And since one can know only what is true, this proposition cannot be known at every time. It cannot be known now. God can know, concerning every temporal event whatsoever, what time that event occurs at, without such knowledge of God's being temporal. But God cannot know concerning any temporal event whatsoever that it is occurring, or know that it was occurring,

39 Augustine, *City of God*, 10.12 (358).

> or know that it will be occurring, without that knowledge being itself temporal.[40]

If God is time-less, God seemingly cannot know time *as time,* for time-lessness and time are mutually exclusive categories. Time-lessness is the strict negation of time, and vice versa. Therefore, if God does not know time, as time, it follows that there is something unknown to God. If there is something unknown to God, then it seems that God is not all-knowing. Wolterstorff feels he must defend God's omniscience against God's alleged time-lessness, and I think he is right to do so; I agree with him.

Plotinus recognized that it is literally impossible for the human mind to conceive of a time-less state of being. This fact is lost on most theologians today. We often hear the illustration that God is like an immovable tree planted by a river, where God is the time-less, unchanging tree and the flowing river next to him is the world of time and change. This metaphor is illusory, however, for in order to imagine the river running beside the tree, we have to imagine the succession inherent to the flowing of a river, but this presupposes time. Thus the metaphor is inadequate.

Sometimes we imagine that God's reality is something like a polaroid photo, in which God sees everything as though in a single still frame. Here again, however, time inevitably creeps into our thinking. When we think about the still frame image, we can only think about it bit by bit, our eyes moving here and there across the image. Thus the *examination* or *observation* of the still frame still necessitates time and succession. If God is able to examine or observe his time-less reality, this still presupposes time. The human mind simply cannot conceive of a time-less state or a time-less mode of being. All thought, as we know it, inevitably presupposes time.

---

40 Wolterstorff, *Inquiring*, 151. Emphasis in original.

To the extent we imagine that God is operative or contemplative in his time-less eternity, we are obviously still sneaking time into our thoughts about God. An "eternal present" seems to amount to little more than the very small amount of time that we allow God to look around and survey his frozen reality.

When advocates of God's time-lessness speak of God's time-less eternity "before time," it seems clear that they are still sneaking time into their thought. They seem to be trying to imagine a God-time that existed "before" man-time, but here they are still stuck thinking in terms of time. They are trying to envision a time before time, as it were. If God is time-less, then it's not any more meaningful to speak of a time-less eternity "before" time than it is to speak of a time-less eternity after time or around the corner from time.

In the *City of God*, Augustine seems to have identified time with physical motion and concluded that before God created creatures to scurry about, there was no time, because there was no physical motion.[41] Yet this would also seemingly rule out *intellectual motion* within God. If God contemplates things, this would seemingly imply a sort of kinetic flow or perpetual, conscious awareness within God's mind, yet this still necessitates time. All thought, contemplation, and awareness, as we know these things, inevitably presuppose time.

Augustine acknowledged that the Bible presents God in time, attributing "years" to God and the like, but he says this is merely a poetic accommodation to the weakness of man.[42] Speaking of biblical terms such as "everlasting" and "forever," Augustine conceded that "by these words Scripture is wont to mean nothing else than endless duration."[43] In other words, Augustine recognized that terms such as "everlasting," in biblical usage, refer only to indefinitely extended time, and not to a time-less state.

41 Augustine, *City of God*, 11.6 (378).

42 See Augustine, *Trinity*, 5.2.9 (195).

43 Augustine, *City of God*, 21.23 (650).

It bears repeating that there is no passage in the Bible which expressly says that God created time, or that God exists outside of time. We have to pose the question, then, where does the doctrine of God's time-lessness come from? Given that the biblical words which speak to God's relationship to time do not imply it (according even to Augustine), and given that it is not stated explicitly in the Bible, the answer to the question obviously cannot be that the doctrine originates from the Bible. In the writings of Augustine, it seems the imperative for the doctrine of God's time-lessness was little more than the alleged theological expertise of the Platonists.

Obviously, the doctrine that time does not apply to God makes God's knowledge radically unlike our own. Clearly, I can't know anything about that sort of knowledge. If God exists outside of time, then all of our knowledge of God becomes unreal and necessarily inapplicable to God himself. God becomes divorced from us. Augustine, in fact, expresses a great deal of concern as to how God, who has no reference to time, can interact with time. "O Lord," he inquires, "since you are outside time in eternity, are you unaware of the things that I tell you? Or do you see in time the things that occur in it?"[44] Since God is time-less and, therefore, does not operate within time, Augustine postulated that God uses angels as intermediaries to operate in time. Angels, in the writings of Augustine, seem to straddle the border of time and time-lessness.

When the Father spoke from heaven and said "This is my beloved Son" (Matthew 3:17), Augustine interpreted this to mean that God used intermediaries to speak, because speaking presupposes time, and the time-less God cannot speak in time:

> From this it is abundantly clear that your speech was expressed through the motion of some created thing, because it was motion subject to the laws of time, although

---

44 Augustine, *Confessions*, 11.1 (112).

> it served your eternal will. These words, which you had caused to sound in time, were reported by the bodily ear of the hearer to the mind, which has intelligence and inward hearing responsible to your eternal Word.[45]

Augustine believed that it was "abundantly clear" that God the Father could not possibly have said "This is my beloved Son" himself, because such words are not simple and they presuppose time. A simple God could hardly speak syllable by syllable, in a manifold, temporal manner. God could not speak like a man because when a man speaks, he speaks bit by bit, part by part, in timely succession, but God has no time, no parts, and no succession. Augustine's position was that God always revealed himself to us only through the intermediaries, especially angels,[46] and cannot reveal himself to us directly. According to Augustine, the time-less God must remain perpetually silent and inoperative in our world of time. This hardly seems to meet the definition of omnipotence, however. Augustine postulated that God always operates in time through the intermediary work of created beings:

> He made use, too, of the words of human speech, uttering them syllable by syllable successively, though in His own nature He speaks not in a bodily but in a spiritual way; not to sense, but to the mind; not in words that occupy time, but, if I may so say, eternally, neither beginning to speak nor coming to an end. And what He says is accurately heard, not by the bodily but by the mental ear of His ministers and messengers, who are immortally blessed in the enjoyment of His unchangeable truth; and the directions which they in some ineffable way receive, they execute without delay or difficulty in the sensible and visible world.[47]

---

45 Augustine, *Confessions*, 11.6 (115).

46 See Augustine, *Trinity*, 3.3-4.

47 Augustine, *City of God*, 10.15 (359).

Much like the Neoplatonists, Augustine's strategy was to multiply intermediaries to ease the tension inherent in the Platonic Divorce between two antithetical modes of being. The proposed solution is entirely inadequate, however. Even an infinite number of intermediary stages would not solve the problem. As we saw in Plotinus, you would still need a moment where this or that creature passed over from time-lessness to time, from simplicity to manifold complexity, but that cannot be because two modes of being mutually exclude one another, *by definition*. Time-lessness and time are mutually exclusive and antithetical, by definition.

Of course, nowhere does the Bible wrestle with the abstruse Neoplatonic question of how time-lessness can interact with time. The Bible is seemingly unaware of the difficulty. My suggestion is that this is because the Bible does not endorse the Platonic doctrine of time-lessness, though many folks undoubtedly read the doctrine into Scripture. In Scripture, God is described as "everlasting" (e.g., Genesis 21:33, Isaiah 40:28, Romans 16:26) precisely because he *lasts* forever. Both the Hebrew and Greek terms refer to a long duration of time and not to a time-less state.[48] The everlasting God presupposes an everlasting duration of time in which to last. God has always existed and he will always exist. God has an infinitely long history. As we look to the past, we understand that God's history is so long as to have no beginning. Likewise, God will continue to endure through time; he will never come to an end. Temporality is not a limitation, but rather the logical precondition of all being, thought, and action.

Augustine argued that the immutable God is entirely passive with regards to human history because a time-less God cannot operate directly in time. Wolterstorff offers a suitable rebuttal:

48 blueletterbible.org is a helpful, free resource where anyone may examine the meaning of the original Hebrew and Greek terms and not take my word for it.

> The biblical writers do not present God as some passive factor within reality but as an agent in it. Further, they present God as acting within *human* history. The god they present is neither the impassive god of the Oriental nor the non-historical god of the deist. Indeed, so basic to the biblical writings is their speaking of God as agent within history that if one viewed God as only an impassive factor in reality, or as one whose agency does not occur within human history, one would have to regard the biblical speech about God as at best one long sequence of metaphors pointing to a reality for which they are singularly inept, and as at worst one long sequence of falsehoods.[49]

Augustine's view of God's relation to space closely paralleled his view of God's relation to time. Since God has no parts, when we say that God is omnipresent, we do not mean that various parts of God can be found in various locations. Rather, *all* of God is everywhere. "He is all in heaven and all on earth."[50] Augustine meant that while God is distinct from his creation, God is nevertheless *exhaustively* everywhere; anywhere we look, God is exhaustively present there. This view is seemingly required by the doctrine of simplicity, for God cannot be *partially* in one space and partially in another. All of the simple God must be in every place, so to speak.

This argument strikes me as unintelligible; for if God is exhaustively at point A (say, to the left of me), then he cannot also exhaustively be at point B (say, to my right), for the two discrete points in space exclude one another. In other words, since point A is not exhaustive of point B, it cannot be true that God is exhaustively at point A and also exhaustively at point B. For neither point A nor point B is exhaustive of the other. Thus, if both propositions are true, they are

---

49 Wolterstorff, *Inquiring*, 133. Emphasis in original.

50 Augustine, *City of God*, 22.29 (692).

both also false. (I'm a little exhausted by my own argument here, but I think it rings true, nevertheless).

Augustine likewise agreed with Plato that God is simple in the Greek philosophical sense of the word. God is identical to each of his predicates such that they are all, in truth, one and the same thing:

> Therefore one and the same thing is being said, whether you say God is eternal or immortal or incorruptible or unchangeable; and again whether you say he is living or understanding, which is the same as wise, the same thing is being said. He has not acquired the wisdom he is wise with, but he is himself wisdom. And this life is the same as the might or power, the same as the beauty, by which he is called powerful or beautiful. ...Again, do goodness and justice differ from each other in God's nature as they do in his works, as though there were two different qualities of God, one goodness, the other justice? Of course not. His justice is the same as his goodness and his goodness the same as his happiness.[51]

Whatever is said of God *is* God. God is not distinct from his own will, nor is he distinct from his own life. God is life itself, life, as such; God is likewise wisdom itself.[52] Augustine was obviously a strong realist about life, wisdom, beauty, and the like. These are not merely useful descriptive terms or practical concepts in the mind, but concrete entities, identical to the being of God. Each of these was imagined to be as concretely real as God himself is; indeed, each of these is nothing more and nothing less than God himself.

Unlike man, God is not distinct from his own thoughts or actions, according to Augustine. God's thinking is identical to his being, which is in turn identical with his love and justice:

---

51 Augustine, *Trinity*, 15.2.7 (400).

52 Augustine, *On Christian Doctrine*, 1.8 (706).

> For to Him it is not one thing to *be*, and another to live, as though He could *be*, not living, nor is it to Him one thing to live, and another thing to understand, as though He could live, not understanding; nor is it to Him one thing to understand, another thing to be blessed, as though He could understand and not be blessed. But to Him to live, to understand, to be blessed, are *to be*. They [the Platonists] have understood, from this unchangeableness and this simplicity, that all things must have been made by Him, and that He could Himself have been made by none.[53]

Though man distinguishes between God's thinking, acting, speaking, creating, loving, being, hating of sin, and the like, such distinctions are unreal for Augustine as far as God-in-himself is concerned. The simple God cannot possess distinctions; God is identical to his attributes such that they are all really one and the same.

Augustine agreed with Clement that God makes accommodations to man by presenting himself, at times, in worldly, human guise. In Scripture, God is said to have eyes, ears, arms, and even wings (e.g., Psalm 17:8), but such representations should not be understood literally. "The scriptures employ no manner of speaking that is not in common human usage—they are, after all, speaking to human beings."[54] God makes accommodations to us so as to help us gradually lift our gaze heavenward. "The divine Scriptures then are in the habit of making something like children's toys out of things that occur in creation, by which to entice our sickly gaze and get us step by step to seek as best we can the things that are above and forsake the things that are below."[55]

---

53 Augustine, *City of God*, 8.6 (316). Emphasis in original.

54 Augustine, *Trinity*, 1.4.23 (83).

55 Augustine, *Trinity*, 1.1.2 (66).

God-in-himself, in his simple unity, has no internal divisions or distinctions. He is identical to his own eternity and to his own eternal situation. Even the creation itself has always been present to God and is, in this sense, one with God:

> So because there is but one Word of God, through which all things were made (Jn 1:1-6), which is unchanging truth, in which all things are primordially and unchangingly together, not only things that are in the whole of this creation, but things that have been and will be; but there it is not a question of "have been" and "will be," there they simply are; and all things there are life and all are one, and indeed there is there but one "one" and one life.[56]

Augustine was certainly no pantheist, yet it seems dangerously Plotinian to say God and creation are alike "one" as far as the simple God is concerned. The difficulty Augustine faced is that if God is aware of a creation totally distinct from himself, then he is most definitely aware of distinctions. Yet a God aware of distinctions quite obviously contains distinctions and is not strictly simple after all. Many other expressions of Augustine seem like they would lead to pantheism if taken seriously. In one place, he wrote, "if a man is full of love, what is he full of but God?"[57] Augustine's thought is that since God is love, as such (understood in a literal, strongly realist sense), then all human expression of love must be identical to the being of God. Likewise, if God is *being*, as such, then all beings would seemingly be identical to the simple being of God. Augustine would shun such conclusions, of course. In the chapter to follow, however, we will see that Dionysius the Areopagite embraced such conclusions with vigor.

---

56 Augustine, *Trinity*, 4.1.3 (154).

57 Augustine, *Trinity*, 8.5.11 (253).

Augustine offered a number of arguments for simplicity in *The City of God*. If God were not simple but were something diverse like a cup full of liquor or a human body and its skin color, God would be changeable.[58] God could, in such a case, be deprived of what he has. Liquor can be poured out of a cup, and the color of our skin can be artificially changed. Likewise, physical bodies and cups of liquor are "greater in whole than in part"[59] but nothing can be greater than God, even within God himself, and so God must be simple. If God were not simple, he would seemingly need some "extraneous supplement"[60] to support him, as the liquor in the glass requires the glass to hold it. God would also need to derive his qualities from external forces or realities and would not be a totally independent being.

Each of these arguments seems to appeal to the character of material objects. A material object can, of course, be broken down into lesser parts. It can be made less or more than it was previously. It can be made smaller than it was previously, in which case it is no longer as "great" as it once was.[61] Material objects are acted on by external forces and, in Christian belief, obtain their being and essential character from external forces.

In the first place, I think we have to allow that we possess very little knowledge about the nature of spiritual objects. Spiritual objects are, of course, not subject to our empirical observation. We really don't know the mechanics, so to speak, of the spiritual world. We really don't know the first thing about it. Scripture conveys to us a bit of practical survival knowledge, but, beyond that, our ignorance of spiritual realities is quite profound. Augustine seems to assume the spiritual realm operates in a manner similar to the physical realm, but is this

58 Augustine, *City of God*, 11.10 (380).

59 Augustine, *City of God*, 11.10 (380).

60 Augustine, *City of God*, 11.10 (381).

61 The argument contains an equivocation as Augustine confuses and conflates the various meanings of the word "great."

assumption well-founded? Need we worry that God will fall to pieces unless we deem him simple?

Simplicity seems to me a safeguard against a very strange sort of heretic. I think everyone will allow that God cannot be taken apart like a puzzle or his attributes poured out like liquor from a glass. I think everyone will concur that God cannot lose what is essential to his character and nature. I think everyone will concede that God does not derive his being or attributes from some external force. Do such assertions really require simplicity, however, wrought as it is with endless perplexities? Like Plato's Forms, the theory creates far more problems than it solves.

Nor was Augustine consistent with the doctrine. Though he is always adamant about the divine simplicity, he allows one definite, explicit exception: God is simple, except that he is a Trinity of persons. "We say [the Trinity] is simple, because it is what it has, with *exception* of the relation of the persons to one another."[62] The difficulty here seemed to be that if the person of the Father, the person of the Son, and the person of the Spirit were the same simple stuff, so to speak, they would seemingly be three identical persons. Yet three identical persons would be totally indistinguishable,[63] and three indistinguishable persons would really only be one person. Augustine seemingly allowed for the awkward exception to save the Trinity from simplicity.

I suspect that Plato and Plotinus would respond by saying that if simplicity admitted any exceptions, it would no longer be simplicity. Simplicity, by definition, means the absence of any and all distinctions. It is patently incoherent to say that God is simple (i.e., possesses no distinctions) but that there is nevertheless a three-fold distinction within God. This was, in fact, a favorite argument of the Arians against the orthodox in the ancient church. If God is a Trinity, then God

62 Augustine, *City of God*, 11.10 (381).

63 Per the law of indiscernibles in formal logic as well as Euclid's "common notions", number one, in mathematics.

must be, according to Arius, "composite and divisible and mutable and a body."[64] Rather than reject the Platonic doctrine of simplicity, the Arians chose to reject the biblical doctrine of the Trinity, demonstrating (in my view, at least) that their commitments were more with Plato's worldly wisdom than with the Bible itself. In truth, we would be hard pressed to find *any* early Christian heresy that didn't wield Plato against Scripture, despite their alleged agreement.

Augustine attributed the Good, Mind, and Soul of Plotinus to Plato, and thereby suggested that Plato had a clear awareness of the Holy Trinity.[65] The Good is identified with the Father, Mind is identified with the Son.[66] Soul is, of course, the Holy Spirit.

Though Plotinus' student Porphyry was an ardent apologist against Christianity, authoring a treatise entitled *Against the Christians* (in an era of intense Christian persecution, no less), this did not stop Augustine from scouring his works for insights into the Father, Son, and Holy Spirit. A small sample should suffice:

> For he [Porphyry] speaks of God the Father and God the Son, whom he calls (writing in Greek) the intellect or mind of the Father; but of the Holy Spirit he says either nothing, or nothing plainly, for I do not understand what other he speaks of as holding the middle place between these two. For if, like Plotinus in his discussions regarding the three principal substances, he wished us to understand by this third the soul of nature, he would certainly not have given it the middle place between these two, that is, between the Father and the Son. For Plotinus places the soul of nature after the intellect of the Father, while Porphyry, making it the mean, does not place it after, but between the others. No doubt he

---

64 Arius, *Epistle to Alexander*, quoted in Pelikan, *Christian Tradition*, 1.194.

65 Copleston, *History*, V2, 30.

66 See Augustine, *City of God*, 10.29 (368).

> spoke according to his light, or as he thought expedient; but we assert that the Holy Spirit is the Spirit not of the Father only, nor of the Son only, but of both.[67]

It is astonishing to see Augustine reading the biblical Holy Trinity into the philosophies of Plotinus and Porphyry. To us these systems seem quite far apart, but that was clearly not the case for Augustine. Just as he was reading Platonism into Scripture, so too he was reading Scripture into the Platonists. Both groups were artificially forced into accord with one another.

Augustine could perhaps be forgiven for identifying the Holy Trinity with Plotinus's three "hypostases" in his youth. Yet this quote is found in his mature thought, written later in his life. It would, perhaps, be plausible to say that there is a knowledge of the Trinity in nature which the Platonists had seen something of. Even so, scouring the works of Plotinus and Porphyry for insight into the biblical doctrine of the Holy Trinity is, so far as I can see, straightforward foolishness. In several places, Augustine went so far as to say that Porphyry worshiped the same God as Christians.[68] Certainly Porphyry, the anti-Christian apologist, would have disagreed!

Even more tragic is the fact that it was on account of an implicit commitment to the Plotinian and Porphyrian models of the "Trinity" that the so-called Greek Orthodox church departed from mainstream orthodoxy in the eleventh century. To this very day, Greek Orthodoxy remains committed to the error that the Spirit does not proceed bilaterally from both the Father and the Son but unilaterally from the Father only, in much the same manner as Plotinus' Soul was imagined to proceed unilaterally from Mind and Mind unilaterally from the Good.

From the start, simplicity fit awkwardly with the doctrine of the Trinity. If God is a Trinity, God cannot be simple, for a simple thing,

67 Augustine, *City of God*, 10.23 (363-364).

68 Augustine, *City of God*, 22.3 (663). See also 22.25 (688).

by definition, admits of no distinction, yet the Trinity doctrine necessitates a threefold distinction internal to God. In whatever sense God is a three-fold Trinity, it follows that he is not simple in that sense.

Even if we allow that each person is merely a single "peculiar quality" within God (a meager allotment indeed!), it still follows that there are a trio of peculiar qualities internal to God. Augustine expended a tremendous amount of energy trying to reconcile simplicity with the doctrine of the Trinity. It is among the most fundamental of his concerns in his lengthy book on the subject. Since God is simple, according to Augustine, we know that he doesn't have a plurality of "attributes," for all of his attributes are identical to one another. When we say things such as "God is great" our speech is inaccurate because God is identical to his greatness in a manner we cannot comprehend. Likewise, we should recognize that all three persons partake in God's indivisible and simple unity:

> So he is great with a greatness by which he is himself this same greatness. And that is why we do not say three greatnesses any more than we say three beings; for God it is the same thing to be as to be great. For the same reason we do not say three great ones but one great one, but God is not great by participating in greatness, but he is great with his great self because he is his own greatness. The same must be said about goodness and eternity and omnipotence and about absolutely all the predications that can be stated of God, because it is all said with reference to himself, and not metaphorically either or in simile but properly—if anything, that is, can be said properly about him by a human tongue.[69]

69 Augustine, *Trinity*, 5.2.11 (196).

Since God's greatness is an absolutely simple unity, identical to God himself, we should not say there are three great persons, but rather that the three persons partake in the one, simple great unity. This is a very awkward distinction. For Augustine, it cannot be said that the Father (or Son or Spirit) is great *in himself,* as a person, but only to the extent that he participates in the one great, simple essence. God is great, but the three persons not so much. This is a very heavy-handed and, indeed, stifling distinction. Even today, it is commonplace for Christian theologians to assert that God is simple and indivisible—without distinction—and yet exists distinctly as Father, Son, and Spirit. This view is manifestly incoherent. Simplicity must ultimately obliterate the three-fold distinction inherent to a Trinity, just as a robust doctrine of the Trinity must ultimately obliterate the pagan doctrine of simplicity.

In Augustine's case, it is clear that he had a strong modalist tendency. Undoubtedly, he would deny the charge, but that does not mean that it has no merit. For all intents and purposes, God is defined by Augustine as one in precisely the same sense that he is defined as being three: "it is not one thing for God *to be* and another for him to be person, but altogether the same."[70] Given simplicity, each person must be identical to God considered as a whole, and thus seemingly identical to each other person. Augustine, in fact, said that the three divine persons, considered collectively, are not anything more or anything in addition to any one person considered individually.[71] That being the case, the conclusion seems to be inescapable that the Father, Son, and Spirit would be indistinguishably one and the same person.

Given that God is simple, time-less, and immutable and that we are none of these things, Augustine allows that we cannot know anything as God knows it:

---

70 Augustine, *Trinity*, 7.3.11 (229).

71 Augustine, *Trinity*, 7.3.11 (230).

> Just as you are perfect being, so you alone have perfect knowledge; for your being, your knowledge, and your will are immutable. Your being knows and wills unchangeably; your knowledge is and wills unchangeably; and your will is and knows unchangeably. In your eyes it does not seem right that a mutable being, illumined by our immutable light, should know that light as the light knows itself.[72]

Augustine's view is that we cannot know anything about God as God knows it. Of course, the God that God knows is the God that actually exists as God. The God that we know would be, in such a case, not God himself, but some sort of infinitely removed caricature.

Augustine sometimes admits that the doctrines of time-lessness and simplicity make God feel distant and unknowable to us. These teachings often seem to us great intellectual roadblocks. He frequently argued that it is on account of our sin that our vision is obscured and we have difficulty understanding and obtaining a clear intellectual grasp of these truths.[73]

Since God is immutable and time-less, according to Augustine, it follows also that God is impassible. God cannot have new emotions any more than he can have new thoughts or perform new actions. God is identical to his own emotional state:

> Only you can never change, because you alone are absolute simplicity, for whom to live is the same as to live in blessed happiness, since you are your own beatitude.[74]

For us humans, our existence is something quite separate and distinguishable from a momentary feeling of happiness. According to Augustine, the same is not true of God. Since God is simple, it is not one

---

72 Augustine, *Confessions*, 13.16 (147).

73 See Augustine, *Trinity*, 4.5.31 (176).

74 Augustine, *Confessions*, 13.3 (141).

thing for God to be happy and another thing for God to exist. Rather, God is identical to happiness and existence, as such. Happiness is, on this account, a personal being. Presumably we may worship Happiness and pray to Happiness, given that God and Happiness are identical.

According to Augustine, God has no diverse moods or emotions. The static God knows nothing of emotional change:

> Indeed, to say that He is affected at all, is an abuse of language, since it implies that there comes to be something in His nature which was not there before. For he who is affected is acted upon, and whatever is acted upon is changeable.[75]

Since God's mode of being is absolutely static, he is capable of neither joy nor sorrow. Augustine insists that Scripture speaks anthropomorphically when it applies joy and sorrow to God. Expressions such as "the wrath of God" in Scripture are always figurative.[76] God is strictly incapable of wrath, for God cannot undergo change. He is "wholly everywhere without place, everlasting without time, without any change in himself making changeable things, and undergoing nothing."[77] Though Scripture says such things as "as a bridegroom rejoices over his bride, so will your God rejoice over you" (Isaiah 62:5), Augustine would undoubtedly view this as an anthropomorphic accommodation. God cannot experience new events and so cannot feel new emotions. Nothing is ever new to God. The immutable God cannot actually temporally rejoice at the temporal salvation of an individual sinner, nor can God get temporarily angry at our sins in time.

Augustine said that though Scripture attributes anger to God, the anger in question should not be viewed as subjectively in God, as if God could be unsettled by the actions of man. Though "even God Himself

---

75 Augustine, *City of God*, 12.17 (408).

76 Augustine, *On Christian Doctrine*, 3.11 (745).

77 Augustine, *Trinity*, 5.Prologue.2 (190).

is said in Scripture to be angry, and yet without any perturbation. For this word is used of the effect of His vengeance, not of the disturbing mental affection."[78] Though Scripture describes God's anger subjectively, as if God experiences the emotion of anger like we do, Augustine believed we should interpret God's anger objectively rather than subjectively. When we read of God's anger, we should understand his objective justice and not any subjective emotions.[79] When we perceive God as angry it is something like a person with an eye injury perceiving the sun to be angry though "in itself it remains the same as it was."[80] Speaking of God's anger, he wrote:

> But if Scripture were not to use such expressions as the above, it would not familiarly insinuate itself into the minds of all classes of men, whom it seeks access to for their good, that it may alarm the proud, arouse the careless, exercise the inquisitive, and satisfy the intelligent; and this could not do, did it not first stoop, and in a manner descend, to them where they lie.[81]

The child and the simpleton may well believe that God gets emotionally angry over sin, but the Christian philosopher knows better. He understands that God's anger should be interpreted in light of the philosophical conviction that anger is a strict impossibility for God. God's temporal anger—constantly spoken of in Scripture—is dismissed on account of God's impassibility, which is nowhere mentioned in Scripture. It should be admitted that this is a curious canon of biblical interpretation.

---

78 Augustine, *City of God*, 9.5 (338).

79 See Augustine, *Trinity*, 13.5.21 (360).

80 Augustine, *City of God*, 22.2 (662).

81 Augustine, *City of God*, 15.25 (479).

Augustine rejected Clement's view that Jesus didn't have any emotions. Jesus experienced emotions in his humanity,[82] though not in his divinity. Augustine also disagreed with Clement that the saints in heaven are free from all emotion. Christians will certainly continue to experience subjective love and joy in heaven.[83]

Similarly, since God is immutable, according to Augustine, it is impossible for God to form any new personal relationships from God's perspective:

> God is called our refuge by way of relationship; the name has reference to us. And he becomes our refuge when we take refuge in him. Does this mean that something happens then in his nature, which was not there before we took refuge in him? No, the change takes place in us; we were worse before we took refuge in him, and we become better by taking refuge in him. *But in him, no change at all.* So too, he begins to be our Father when we are born again by his grace, because He gave us the right to become sons of God (John 1:12). So our substance changes for the better when we are made his sons; at the same time he begins to be our Father, but without any change in his substance. So it is clear that anything that can begin to be said about God in time which was not said about him before is said by way of relationship, and yet not by way of a modification of God, as though something has modified him....That a just man begins to be called the friend of God means that he changes. *But it is unthinkable that God should love someone temporally, as though with a new love that was not in him before*, seeing that with him things past do not pass, and things future have already happened. So he loved all his saints before the

82 Augustine, *City of God*, 14.9 (441).

83 Augustine, *City of God*, 14.9 (441).

> foundation of the world (John 17:24; Ephesians 1:4), and he predestined them; but when they are converted and find him, then they are said to begin to be loved by him, in order to state the thing in a way that can be grasped by human feeling. So too when he is said to be angry with the wicked and pleased with the good, they change, not he; just as light is harsh to weak eyes, pleasant to strong; but it is the eyes, not the light, that change.[84]

When a human is saved, a new relationship is obviously formed from the human perspective. We begin to cry out to God. Yet from God's perspective, according to Augustine, no change has occurred. God's perspective is as immutable and time-less as his being. Indeed, his perspective is identical to his being. God cannot personally relate to me now any more than he did before my birth. Though salvation brings about a change in man, God is not subject to change and is, thus, not cognizant of temporal changes. "For God does not see in time, nor does anything new happen in his sight or his knowledge when some temporal and transitory action is performed."[85]

Such a teaching seems to present countless difficulties for biblical interpretation. If there is no change of relationship from God's point of view when a person is saved, then my salvation in time seems quite illusory and unreal. From God's time-less point of view, I was presumably always saved, and I was always God's child. My personal acceptance or nonacceptance in time seems to matter little in such a scheme. Temporal human history becomes unreal.

If I may again interject as the simpleton that I am, if I should come to believe that God doesn't get angry with my particular sins in time, and is entirely unaffected by my sin at an emotional level, I should naturally feel much more at liberty to sin freely. The sinner in

---

84 Augustine, *Trinity*, 5.4.17 (201).

85 Augustine, *Trinity*, 7.3.10 (328).

me is quite thrilled to discover that God isn't actually bothered by my sins! Seemingly, God is not even aware of my sins here in time. If the time-less and impassible God cannot be bothered by my sin, then why should I be much bothered?

God is absolutely unresponsive at an emotional level for Augustine. The impetus behind the doctrine was obviously not the Bible, which quite plainly describes God as highly emotional. The impetus must be found elsewhere. Emotions are weaknesses for Augustine and, as one contemporary author has noted, "Augustine is merely continuing the philosophical tradition of Platonic and Stoic sensibilities."[86] Wolterstorff similarly concludes his study of Augustine's view of impassibility by noting, "the Augustinian God turns out to be remarkably like the Stoic sage: devoid of passions, unfamiliar with longing, foreign to suffering, dwelling in steady bliss, exhibiting to others only benevolence."[87]

Augustine generally agreed with Clement that man's physical desires are evil. He lamented that he sometimes found pleasure in eating and drinking.[88] Food and drink are only for the fulfillment of need and should not be enjoyed. Sex is only for procreation, and never for pleasure; even to lust after your own wife is a sin.[89] Augustine preferred chants to singing, for sometimes musical melodies are pleasurable to our ears and that is a sin.[90] We are not to enjoy the music, but only to listen carefully to the words. The famously monotonous Gregorian chants of the medieval era were born out of this mentality. The general enjoyment of sensory experience is, according to Augustine, what the Bible means by the lust of the eyes.[91] According to Copleston,

86 Castelo, *Apathetic*, 59.

87 Wolterstorff, *Inquiring*, 199.

88 Augustine, *Confessions*, 10.31 (103).

89 Augustine, *On Christian Doctrine*, 3.20 (748).

90 See Augustine, *Confessions*, 10.33 (105).

91 See Augustine, *Confessions*, 10.35 (107).

> [Augustine's] outlook is markedly Platonic in character. There is the same depreciation of sense-objects in comparison with eternal and immaterial realities, the same almost grudging admission of practical knowledge as a necessity of life, the same insistence on 'theoretic' contemplation, the same insistence on increasing purification of soul and liberation from the slavery of the senses to accompany the epistemological ascent.[92]

In light of his classical theism, Augustine recognized a breakdown of communication between God and man, because man cannot think about God in simple terms:

> Our knowledge therefore is vastly dissimilar to this knowledge. What is God's knowledge is also his wisdom, and what is his wisdom is also his being or substance, because in the wonderful simplicity of that nature it is not one thing to be wise, another to be, but being wise is the same as being, as we have already said often enough in previous books. But our knowledge, as regards most of its objects, can be both lost and acquired for the very reason that for us to be is not the same thing as to know or to be wise, since we can be, even if we do not know and are not wise to things we have learnt from elsewhere. That is why...our knowledge is so dissimilar to that knowledge of God.[93]

Augustine allowed that God-in-himself is, in the last analysis, unknowable to us. In truth, "no words of ours are capable of expressing him."[94] Elsewhere he wrote, "The total transcendence of the godhead quite surpasses the capacity of ordinary speech. God can be thought

---

92 Copleston, *History*, V2, 58.

93 Augustine, *Trinity*, 15.4.22 (414).

94 Augustine, *Trinity*, 5.Prologue.1 (189).

about more truly than he can be talked about, and he *is* more truly than he can be thought about."[95]

Augustine recounted that the Platonists convinced him that man exists on a lower tier of reality than God, and that man is, in a sense, unreal:

> I considered all the other things that are of a lower order than yourself, and I saw that they have not absolute being in themselves, nor are they entirely without being. They are real in so far as they have their being from you, but unreal in the sense that they are not what you are.[96]

God is *being*. Man is *becoming*. In accepting numerous elements of the Platonic and Neoplatonic outlook, Augustine clearly embraced the Platonic Divorce. God and man are seen as being on two entirely different planes of being, with no possible epistemic overlap or similarity. We find in Augustine the same implicit distinction that we saw in Clement between God-in-himself and God-as-revealed. God is in the upper sphere. Man is in the lower sphere. No contact between the two is possible, because God and man have been *defined* as polar opposites in a dualistic scheme. I won't bore you with the same diagram yet again; the reader may refer to the earlier diagrams. God becomes unknowable and UNKNOWN in such a scheme. Augustine embraced Plato's dilemma. The Platonic structure of reality—in two disparate modes—is embraced as biblical still today. Indeed, it is demanded by the confessions of Rome and of the Reformation alike.

Once again, I can only lament that the design of the present work drew us into a discussion of Augustine's shortcomings rather than his strengths. I have written of some of his strengths elsewhere.[97] Despite

---

95 Augustine, *Trinity*, 7.3.7 (225).

96 Augustine, *Confessions*, 7.1 (61).

97 In *The Secret of Sacrificial Self-Service*, for instance, I explore Augustine's view of the proper place of self-interest and self-denial in the life of the Christian.

his shortcomings, Augustine's writings demonstrate profound insight and compelling spiritual growth. As he matured, his views became notably less Platonic and (in my view) notably more biblical. No Christian before him probed as deeply or as perceptively into the nature of sin and evil, free will and predestination, egoism and altruism, and a host of other theological and philosophical issues.

Augustine served as the Bishop of the city Hippo Regius (in what is today Algeria, Africa) for thirty-five years. He died of illness in 430 AD, as Germanic Vandals were besieging the Roman city.

7

DIONYSIUS THE AREOPAGITE

THE Apostle Paul preached his sermon to the worshippers of the UNKNOWN GOD at a large rock outcropping in Athens. The pagans had dedicated the site to their god of war. To the Romans, he was known as Mars, where the Greeks knew him as Ares. Thus, the location was called "Mars Hill" by the Romans and the "Areopagus" (literally, "hill of Ares") by the Greeks. A man named Dionysius was converted to Christianity after hearing the Apostle's sermon (see Acts 17:34).

A number of works attributed to Dionysius circulated throughout the Middle Ages, including several addressed to the Apostle Paul's other pupil, Timothy. A few were even addressed to John the Apostle. Though some questioned the authenticity of these writings, they were generally accepted as authentic up through the time of the Renaissance. Pope Martin I (600–655 AD), for example, appealed to the writings as authentic.[1]

---

1 Copleston, *History*, V2, 91.

Since these works were thought to be from the first century and from the pen of a close associate of Paul, they enjoyed an immense readership. It was thought that perhaps it was this same associate of the Apostle who had written the anonymous letter to the Hebrews. Therefore, it was easy to place the authority of Dionysius on par with that of the Apostle Paul and Holy Scripture.

Today we know that the author of these works lived no less than three centuries after the Dionysius who had been converted under the ministry of Paul. Unfortunately, we do not know who actually wrote them or what motivated the fantastic hoax. The writer—clearly very educated—went to great lengths over the course of a dozen works (most of which are now lost) to never break character and to avoid any possible hint that he was, in fact, born later than he claimed. By and large, he strikes his readers as sincere in his devotion to Jesus Christ and the God of Holy Scripture. I would like to think that his motives—whatever they may have been—were of a pure rather than a profane sort. However, all opinions on the subject are mere conjecture.

Today, the writer formerly known as Dionysius the Areopagite is commonly referred to as "Pseudo-Dionysius" in recognition of the fact that he is not actually the Dionysius mentioned in the Bible. I will continue to call him Dionysius not because I allow that the works are authentic, but simply because it is important for us to appreciate the fact that the bulk of medieval Christians believed him to be the very same figure mentioned in the book of Acts.

It now seems probable that Dionysius was a student of Proclus (c. 410–485 AD) who was the head of Plato's Academy in Athens for nearly fifty years. Though not a particularly original thinker, Proclus was an extensive systematizer and commentator on the works of Plato and Plotinus.

Though Dionysius is of marginal interest in the history of philosophy, his historical influence on Christian theology was immense. For the better part of a thousand years these works were read as authoritative.

The sheer number of quotations of Dionysius in the works of Thomas Aquinas, for example, some 800 years later, make it clear that Dionysius was still viewed as an authoritative—if not divinely inspired—writer. Additionally, we will see that many of Aquinas' most important philosophical distinctions came directly from Dionysius.

Since Dionysius was believed to be a disciple of Paul, and since he wrote in the language of Platonism, these works greatly reinforced and solidified the view of Clement and Augustine that Platonism and Christianity were close allies which taught nearly the same set of truths about God. Dionysius was undoubtedly a classical theist. Like Clement and Augustine, he claimed that God is the time-less author of time:

> Almighty God we ought to celebrate, both as eternity and time, as Author of every time and eternity, and "Ancient of days," as before time, and above time; and as changing appointed seasons and times; and again as being before ages, in so far as He is both before eternity and above eternity and His kingdom, a kingdom of all the Ages.[2]

Since God is also simple, it's not completely accurate to say that God is eternal; rather, "He is eternity itself."[3]

Dionysius made a fundamental distinction between Mystic Theology and Symbolic Theology.[4] Mystic Theology deals with God as he is, in himself. Since God-in-himself is strictly time-less and simple, Dionysius inferred that God is outside of our intellectual comprehension. Our knowledge of God-in-himself is, therefore, purely apophatic. We have no positive knowledge of God-in-himself; Mystic Theology, therefore, deals only in negations. We can only say what God-in-himself is not.

---

2 Dionysius, *Divine Names*, 10.3 (75).

3 Dionysius, *Divine Names*, 5.10 (56).

4 See Dionysius, *Mystic Theology*, Preface (88).

Symbolic Theology, on the other hand, describes God in terms that accommodate our finite, creaturely understanding; such is the nature of biblical revelation. Positive affirmations are undoubtedly made about God in Scripture, but these affirmations are made through human language, in human symbols, and portray God through creaturely metaphors and analogies. Scripture is molded and shaped to accommodate man's limited understanding.[5]

Thus, according to Dionysius, our knowledge of God is strictly limited to creaturely symbols and creaturely analogies. He tells us that Scripture itself teaches us that God-in-himself is unknowable:

> Concerning this then, as has been said, the superessential and hidden Deity, it is not permitted to speak or even to think beyond the things divinely revealed to us in the sacred Oracles [i.e., the Bible]. For even as Itself has taught (as becomes Its goodness) in the Oracles, the science and contemplation of Itself in Its essential Nature is beyond the reach of all created things, as towering superessentially above all.[6]

Sadly, Dionysius fails to give us the biblical reference wherein God discloses that God is beyond disclosure. The sharp distinction he draws here is quite clear, however. Given that God-in-himself is beyond our intellectual reach at even the most fundamental of levels, our knowledge of God is wholly and exclusively limited to creaturely symbols and analogies. Beyond those symbols and analogies which the Scriptural oracles afford us, we are not permitted to tread. According to Dionysius, Mystic Theology and Symbolic Theology are in logical accord with one another, given that the former says we have no positive knowledge of God-in-himself and the latter says we have a

---

5 Dionysius, *Heavenly Hierarchy*, 2.1 (150).

6 Dionysius, *Divine Names*, 1.2 (9).

knowledge of God that is purely accommodative and couched entirely in anthropomorphic metaphors.

The reader will again note that the usage of the pronoun "It" in reference to God is foreign to Scripture but was normative among the Neoplatonists. God is seemingly viewed as far too impersonal and unknown to be a "he." God is, according to Dionysius, "the super-unutterable and super-unknown Isolation."[7]

Given that God-in-himself is wholly beyond our intellectual grasp, we must content ourselves with the biblical revelation which speaks of God in positive—albeit human—terms:

> In addition to these things, we must examine how we know God, Who is neither an object of intellectual nor of sensible perception, nor is absolutely anything of things existing. *Never, then, is it true to say, that we know God*; not from His own nature (for that is unknown, and surpasses all reason and mind), but, from the ordering of all existing things, as projected from Himself, and containing a sort of images and similitudes of His Divine exemplars, we ascend, as far as we have power, to that which is beyond all... And He is neither conceived, nor expressed, nor named. And He is not any of existing things, nor is He known in any one of existing things. And He is all in all, and nothing in none. And He is known to all, from all, and to none from none. For, we both say these things correctly concerning God, and He is celebrated from all existing things, according to the *analogy* of all things, of which He is Cause.[8]

Though creaturely symbols are derived, ultimately, from God as author and exemplar of all things that exist, such symbols nevertheless

7 Dionysius, *Divine Names*, 2.4 (17).

8 Dionysius, *Divine Names*, 7.3 (62).

inevitably fall short of properly depicting God as he is, for all human terminology necessarily falls short of divine simplicity and time-lessness. God-in-himself is "inexpressible, and unknowable, and altogether unrevealed."[9] No knowledge of God, as God, is possible. Dionysius believed that "It is not possible either to express or to conceive what the One, the Unknown, the Super-essential self-existing Good is."[10] He is "above all affirmation and abstraction."[11] God is "the Good" which is "above conception" and "above word."[12] God is "superessentiality above reason and mind and essence."[13]

Dionysius tells us that God-in-himself is properly spoken of only in the negative. Biblical denials about God such as his invisibility and infinity (i.e., the negation of visibility and finitude) are "more appropriate" than what the Bible positively affirms about God.[14] Dionysius would prefer that Scripture speak more like the Platonists.

For Dionysius, all creatures "participate" in the divine life inasmuch as God showers his own qualities upon creation. For example, where the simple God is identical to Being itself, all lesser beings clearly have some participation in *being* as well: "Almighty God is superessentially Being, but the Being is bequeathed to things being."[15] Dionysius' opinion is that to the extent I am *a being*, and to the extent that I am in possession *of being*, I must obviously be a participant in Being, where God is Being itself. As in the case of Being, so too in the case of Beauty:

> We call beautiful that which participates in Beauty; but beauty, the participation of the beautifying Cause of all the beautiful things. But, the superessential Beautiful is called

9 Dionysius, *Divine Names*, 5.1 (51).

10 Dionysius, *Divine Names*, 1.5 (12).

11 Dionysius, *Divine Names*, 2.4 (17).

12 Dionysius, *Divine Names*, 1.1 (9).

13 Dionysius, *Divine Names*, 1.1 (8).

14 Dionysius, *Heavenly Hierarchy*, 2.3 (152).

15 Dionysius, *Divine Names*, 2.11 (22).

> Beauty, on account of the beauty communicated from Itself to all beautiful things, in a manner appropriate to each...[16]

Dionysius reasons, along Platonic and Neoplatonic lines, that since God is Beauty itself, all beautiful things must participate, in some sense, in God, inasmuch as their beauty is necessarily derivative of God's beauty. If God is Beauty as such, seemingly there is no beauty but God's beauty. Likewise, God is Greatness itself and his Greatness "imparts itself to all things great."[17] All goodness, life, being, beauty, greatness, and every other positive quality we observe in the world are likewise derivative of God as the supreme paradigm of all things.

For Dionysius, our beauty is derived from God's Beauty, our life from his Life, our being from his Being, but we must remind ourselves that our understanding of these things does not perfectly parallel God's simple understanding of them. Though they are each inevitably derived from God, something is inevitably lost in translation as we are neither simple nor time-less like God. All humans have a measure of beauty, of course, but it would be odd—if not altogether meaningless—to say that so-and-so *is beauty itself.*

Taking "beauty" in the human sense of the word, we must both affirm and deny that God is beautiful. It is "our duty both to attribute and affirm all the attributes of things existing to It, as Cause of all, and more properly to deny them all to It, as being above all, and not to consider the negations to be in opposition to the affirmations..."[18] Symbolic Theology teaches that our beauty is derived from God's beauty and that our beauty is, therefore, symbolic of his beauty. We may thus praise God for his beauty, but should simultaneously understand that the predication is not strictly appropriate to God, considered in himself.

---

16 Dionysius, *Divine Names*, 4.7 (32).

17 Dionysius, *Divine Names*, 9.2 (69).

18 Dionysius, *Mystic Theology*, 1.2 (90).

Mystic Theology, at the same time, denies that the beauty we know is like God's beauty, for the beauty we know is neither simple nor timeless. In short, we are only able to speak about God in a human way, as if he were a human (Symbolic Theology), where God-in-himself is wholly outside of our comprehension and we can do no better than to make a few apophatic negations (Mystic Theology).

Since our knowledge of God is derived exclusively from creatures, anyone who thinks they understood or saw something of God-in-himself was simply confused or mistaken: "And, if any one, having seen God, understood what he saw, he did not see Him, but some of His creatures that are existing and known."[19]

Since nothing is known of God-in-himself, then, even in the incarnation of Christ mankind could not see Christ's deity, properly speaking. We could only see his humanity:

> But, He is hidden, even after the manifestation, or to speak more divinely, even in the manifestation, for in truth this of Jesus has been kept hidden, and the mystery with respect to Him has been reached by no word nor mind, but even when spoken, remains unsaid, and when conceived [remains] unknown.[20]

If Dionysius is to be trusted on this point, it would seemingly be impossible to escape the conclusion that when men and women in the Bible thought they recognized Jesus' divinity through his miracles, transfiguration, profound teachings, etc., they were mistaken in each instance.

Dionysius taught that the Symbolic Theology is better suited to amateurs in the faith, where the Mystical Theology is for the mature.[21] Since Mystic Theology cannot say anything positively about

---

19 Dionysius, *Letter 1 to Gaius Therapeutes*, (98).

20 Dionysius, *Letter 3 to Gaius Therapeutes,* (99).

21 See Dionysius, *Letter 11 to Titus,* (113).

God-in-himself, however, Dionysius' book on the subject runs only a few pages in length. The shortness of the work was clearly intentional on the part of the author, the whole point being that nothing can be properly said about God. For Dionysius, Christian intellectual maturity seems to end, ironically, in an awkward silence on the subject of who God is. No positive assertions can be made about God-in-himself.

Given his extensive borrowing of the language, metaphors, and tropes of Neoplatonism, it is not surprising that Dionysius has often been charged with pantheism. The Neoplatonic notion that creatures "participate" in God's attributes certainly leaves him open to the charge. It surely grates upon orthodox ears to hear that man is a "participant" in God's life, being, beauty, etc.

Dionysius' cosmology is likewise suggestive of pantheism. It bears a marked similarity to that of Plotinus. Never does he speak of God creating the world willfully, by arbitrary fiat. This would, after all, suggest change and mutability within God. His consistent presentation is, rather, that of natural process. As in Plotinus, the most frequent metaphors are that of the overflowing fountain and the sun naturally and involuntarily shedding forth its rays. Creation is viewed as a sort of unfolding "projection" or "generation" or "multiplication" or "progression" out of God.[22] The Good "benignly sheds forth its superessential ray."[23] The created order is imagined to be a natural by-product or necessary overflow of God's being:

> Further, it may be boldly said with truth, that even the very Author of all things, by reason of *overflowing* Goodness, loves all, makes all, perfects all, sustains all, attracts all; and even the Divine Love is Good of Good, by reason of the Good. For Love itself, the benefactor of things that be, pre-existing *overflowingly* in the Good, did not permit

---

22 See Dionysius, *Divine Names*, 5.1 (51), and 6.3 (58)

23 Dionysius, *Divine Names*, 1.2 (9).

> itself to remain unproductive in itself, but moved itself to creation, as befits the *overflow* which is generative of all.[24]

As in Augustine, a new, willful action on God's part would be a change in God, but God does not change. God is absolutely immutable. Presumably when God "moved itself to creation," it was an involuntary movement, a "generative" overflow. God is, as it were, the "Sovereign root" of creation.[25]

Dionysius' ethic likewise bears a striking similarity to that of Plotinus. It is through intellectual contemplation that man undertakes the Christian journey of "sacred deification."[26] As we become more god-like, we become less passionate, for "the variableness of many passions" is a product of the fall of man.[27] As we progress on our intellectual journey toward God, we move from material conceptions about God (God as a strong warrior, God as a roaring lion, etc.) to abstract, anthropomorphic conceptions (God as loving, long-suffering, wise, etc.), to negative, apophatic conceptions (God as without time, without parts, without passions), arriving ultimately at an understanding that God *in himself* cannot be known at all.

As in Plotinus, the journey ends in a mystical vision where man discards his knowledge (and even his being) to attain momentary union with God:

> This then be my prayer; but thou, O dear Timothy, by thy persistent commerce with the mystic visions, leave behind both sensible perceptions and intellectual efforts, and all objects of sense and intelligence, and all things not being and being, and be raised aloft unknowingly to the union,

24 Dionysius, *Divine Names*, 4.10 (35).

25 Dionysius, *Divine Names*, 10.1 (74).

26 Dionysius, *Ecclesiastical Hierarchy*, 1.2 (195).

27 Dionysius, *Ecclesiastical Hierarchy*, 3.11 (214).

> as far as attainable, with Him Who is above every essence and knowledge.[28]

Seemingly, the only way to know God in a Platonic scheme is to become God. "Those who are being saved are being deified. Now the assimilation to, and union with, God, as far as attainable, is deification."[29] In fairness to Dionysius, he generally qualifies such statements by saying this union is not total but only "as far as attainable" and the like. Still, both the illustrations and the verbiage are often highly aberrant from the standpoint of Christian orthodoxy.

Dionysius agreed with Augustine that angels occupy an intermediary position between God and man. Where all of our reasoning is little by little, word by word, and part by part, angels are able to think in simple terms like God does. Angels do not think "...in portions, or from portions, or sensible perceptions, or detailed reasonings, or arguing from something common to these things, but purified from everything material and multitudinous, they contemplate the conceptions of Divine things intuitively, immaterially and uniformly."[30] Like Plotinus, Dionysius imagined a hierarchy of being in which creatures higher up on the hierarchy possess being, knowledge, life, etc. in a higher measure and to a higher degree. Angels are the most like God because they are nearest to God on the hierarchy of being. They possess more "being" than man possesses, having a higher degree of participation in God's being.

The medieval preoccupation with angels (leading, anecdotally, to the infamously silly question "how many angels can dance on the head of a pin?") was, in large part, due to the necessity of having intermediary stages between the simple God and non-simple man. Angels became the intermediaries between the upper and lower modes of

28 Dionysius, *Mystic Theology*, 1.1 (89).

29 Dionysius, *Ecclesiastical Hierarchy*, 1.3 (196).

30 Dionysius, *Divine Names*, 7.2 (60).

being. Angels became brokers and mediators in the dualistic antithesis of the Platonic divorce. Angels were imagined to straddle the border of time and time-lessness, and of simplicity and manifold complexity. Of course, this was not actually a solution to the problem, but merely a deferral of the exact same problem to a different, more obscure location.

Dionysius clearly held Scripture in high regard, but he believed that the Scriptures speak of God only in symbolic, accommodating metaphors. Though God is depicted in Scripture as thinking, acting, emoting, etc., in a manner similar to us, Dionysius was convinced that God, in himself, is altogether unlike us. God is above and beyond existence as we know it and thus cannot be known. "For, if all kinds of knowledge are of things existing, and are limited to things existing, that, beyond all essence, is also elevated above all knowledge."[31] It would seemingly follow from this that even the assertion that "God exists" is not strictly applicable to God-in-himself inasmuch as God-in-himself is beyond all essence and all existence as we know it.

Dionysius imagined that the well-trained philosopher perceives that behind the passible, temporal, manifold portrayal of God in Scripture is found the real God who is impassible, time-less, and simple. One must study Scripture only to transcend Scripture by reading between the lines. Assertions about God in the Bible should, therefore, never be taken in a strictly literal sense. For Dionysius, Scripture contains an extended human metaphor about a God that is, ultimately, wholly unknown to us. Following Plato, Dionysius was trapped in a dualistic scheme whereby God's knowledge and man's knowledge had been defined as mutually exclusive.

Dionysius was quite clear that God has the same epistemic isolation problem that man does. Just as man knows God only through his knowledge of man, that is, by way of human metaphors, so too God only knows man through his knowledge of God:

31 Dionysius, *Divine Names*, 1.4 (11).

> For not as learning existing things from existing things, does the Divine Mind know, but from Itself, and in Itself, as Cause, it pre-holds and pre-comprehends the notion and knowledge, and essence of all things; not approaching each several thing according to its kind, but knowing and containing all things, within one grasp of the Cause; just as the light, as cause, presupposes in itself the notion of darkness, not knowing the darkness otherwise than from the light.[32]

God knows our change only within the bounds of his entire absence of change. He knows our time only in the context of his time-lessness. God cannot know time *as time* any more than we can know time-lessness *as time-lessness*. The divorce is comprehensive. God seemingly knows nothing of us as we actually are, nor do we know anything of God as "it" is:

> It is neither soul, nor mind, nor has imagination, or opinion, or reason, or conception...nor do things existing know It, as It is; nor does It know existing things, *qua* existing; neither is there expression of It, nor name, nor knowledge....nor truth; neither is there any definition of all of It, nor any abstraction.[33]

Just as we must distinguish between God-in-himself and God-as-known-to-us, so too God must seemingly distinguish between man-in-himself and man-as-known-to-God. For Dionysius, man is trapped in the cave of time and flux, without any direct access to the time-less God, and God is likewise trapped in a cave of time-less, static, motionlessness without any direct access to time. Since God and man have been defined antithetically, neither has access to the thoughts of the other, at least not in the same manner.

---

32 Dionysius, *Divine Names*, 7.2 (61).

33 Dionysius, *Mystic Theology*, 5.1 (95).

Ultimately, Dionysius offers us no hope of discovering anything about God as he actually is. He repeatedly insisted that we know nothing about God, as God. For Dionysius, man's knowledge of God is ultimately only a knowledge of man. The God of the Bible is God presented in a metaphorical, humanized form, but we know that God—the real God—is altogether unlike us because he is simple and time-less. The God of the Bible is, on this account, merely a metaphor about ourselves. The God of the Bible, in Dionysius' Neoplatonic scheme, seems little more than an *authorized idolatry*.

Dionysius, like Clement and Augustine, accepted the Platonic premise that reality consists of two distinct, antithetical modes. Having embraced the dualistic structure of the Platonic metaphysic, they each inherited the same conceptual problems and reached the same skeptical conclusion, namely, that God is beyond predication, unknowable and UNKNOWN.

Despite his errors, Dionysius took a decidedly Christian stand on many issues. He does well to reject the Platonic denigration of the physical body. Bodies, in themselves, are not the cause of sin.[34] Matter, in itself, is not evil. Evil is not a *thing* at all, but a moral failure and a certain lack of goodness.[35] Dionysius, like Augustine, seems to have been a nominalist regarding sin. Sin is not a being or concrete thing but merely a moral failure or shortcoming. Sin has no *being* but is something more like a concept or intellectual assessment. Sin is a genuine offense against God, to be sure, but an *offense* is not a thing, but only a sort of disposition or frame of mind.

Dionysius affirmed the resurrection of physical bodies and maintained that Christ currently possesses a glorified physical body. He affirmed man's original uprightness and fall from grace in the garden. He affirmed the Trinity and the Incarnation—however ineffable—of the unknowable God in the knowable humanity of Christ.

---

34 See Dionysius, *Divine Names*, 4.28 (46).

35 See Dionysius, *Divine Names*, 4.32 (49).

8

Thomas Aquinas

THE establishment of the university system was perhaps the greatest cultural contribution of the medieval world. The University of Bologna was established in 1088, with universities in Salerno, Paris, and Oxford soon to follow. University libraries quickly became warehouses of knowledge; countless works that had been lost for centuries were rediscovered. One such recovery was the philosophical writings of Aristotle, which were re-introduced to Europe, from Muslim sources, in the late twelfth and early thirteenth centuries. Especially after 1160 AD, they became widely available.[1] This was the first time in European history that Aristotle was widely viewed as a great philosopher in his own right.

These works were met with strong resistance at first. In 1210, for example, the University of Paris ordered Aristotle's texts to be burnt. In 1215, the prohibition was renewed, suggesting that the first had not been followed.[2] Though reinforced by papal authority, this prohibition was ineffective. By 1255, the very same works were a part of the

1 Colish, *Medieval*, 286.

2 Colish, *Medieval*, 289.

school's core syllabus, mandated as essential learning.[3] Intellectual tides can clearly turn very quickly.

Thomas Aquinas (1225-1274) is considered the greatest of the medieval Scholastic philosophers. Born into feudal nobility, he was sent by his father to be raised by Benedictine monks at age five. He joined the monastic order of the Dominicans in 1244. By many accounts, he created the perfect synthesis of Greek philosophy and orthodox Christian theology. Of course, the impulse to synthesize Greek philosophy and Christian theology was Aquinas' inheritance rather than his invention. Scholastic philosophers represented merely another phase in the development of the ancient *synthesis bias* whereby Christian thinkers felt it incumbent upon them to reconcile Scripture with the world's esteemed philosophies.

Though Aquinas is well-known as a disciple of Aristotle, the influence of Platonism upon his thought should not be overlooked. Where Plato had looked to a hidden, otherworldly realm for knowledge, Aristotle emphasized the acquisition of knowledge through observation of the concrete, material world. Knowledge is acquired not by escaping into the deep recesses of the mind but by physical sensation and observation of concrete substances (i.e., physical objects and creatures) in the material world. Where Plato had a decidedly ethereal, spiritual tone, Aristotle strikes us as a man of science and as a materialist. Countless commentators throughout the centuries believed that Aristotle rejected the ideas of personal immortality and of the afterlife, though it remains a matter of debate.

Aquinas could hardly build a comprehensive system of *Christian* thought upon a strictly Aristotelian foundation; Plato filled the gaps that remained. Anthony Kenny is, therefore, not wrong in describing Aquinas as "an Aristotelian on earth, but a Platonist in heaven."[4] William Inge went so far as to say that, "To me at least it is clear that St.

---

3 Kenny, *History*, V2, 300. Also, Luscombe, *Medieval*, 76.

4 Kenny, *History*, V2, 408. Emphasis in original.

Thomas is nearer to Plotinus than to the *real* Aristotle."[5] Once again, I agree with Inge.

To cite one important example, Aquinas, like Augustine, placed the Forms inside the mind of God.[6] The Forms are the eternal pattern by which God created the world. This is an important divergence from the view of Aristotle, who did not teach that the Forms were in the mind of God, and, in fact, did not believe in a free creation of the world by God. According to Copleston, "St. Thomas is therefore following in the wake of the tradition which began with Plato, was developed in Middle Platonism and neo-Platonism and lived on, in a Christian setting, in the philosophy of Augustine and those who followed him."[7]

Aquinas taught that man acquires knowledge in three distinct ways. We can loosely characterize them as natural reason, divine revelation, and heavenly glorification. His view was that while man acquires a small amount of knowledge about God through the powers of his natural reason, this knowledge is generally insufficient for salvation. Man obtains a much better knowledge of God, both quantitatively and qualitatively, through divine revelation. While both human reason and divine revelation are valid sources of human knowledge about God, in neither case do we achieve a knowledge of God in his essence. For Aquinas, it is only in our heavenly glory that we finally attain some knowledge of God-in-himself.

Where philosophy, according to Aquinas, is concerned with the ability of the natural reason to attain truth, unaided by external authority, theology concerns those truths revealed directly by God in Holy Scripture. Philosophy and theology are thus each valid disciplines concerning distinct subjects.

---

5 Inge, *Plotinus*, V1, 15. Emphasis in original.

6 See Aquinas, *Summa Theologica*, 1.15.1, reply to objection 1

7 Copleston, *History*, V2, 359.

Using only natural reason, philosophers can discover many truths about God and nature, but they can also err and the system of truth they discover can never be comprehensive. Reason, by itself, can only get us so far. "Therefore," says Aquinas, "in order that the salvation of men might be brought about more fitly and more surely, it was necessary that they should be taught divine truths by divine revelation."[8]

Scripture is needed to attain infallible truth, though the divine authority must be accepted by faith. Faith in the authority of Scripture is the first principle of theological science, and the first principles of any discipline are not capable of strict logical demonstration.[9] Though faith cannot be proven by reason, strictly speaking, it is in general accord with reason, and it is certainly impossible to disprove.[10] Christians believe, by faith, that theology is the highest science because it concerns the highest subject, namely, God, and is granted to man with infallible authority and complete accuracy.[11] Some truths of revelation, such as the Holy Trinity, cannot be acquired through natural reason, but require divine revelation.[12]

Though canonical Scripture[13] is infallible, philosophers and the great theologians of the church can make mistakes and, therefore, always deal in mere probabilities.[14] Though a given passage of Scripture may be applied in various ways, the literal sense of Scripture is the foundation of all other applications and methods of interpretation:

8 Aquinas, *Summa Theologica*, 1.1.1. Notice that the quote leaves open the possibility that philosophy could possibly bring about salvation. Scripture merely provides a more sure way.

9 Aquinas, *Summa Theologica*, 1.1.8.

10 Aquinas, *Summa Theologica*, 1.1.8.

11 Aquinas, *Summa Theologica*, 1.1.5.

12 See Aquinas, *Summa Theologica*, 1.12.13.

13 In which Aquinas appears to include the Apocrypha.

14 Aquinas, *Summa Theologica*, 1.1.8.

"Hence it is plain that nothing false can ever underlie the literal sense of Holy Writ."[15]

We know that the existence of God is not self-evident to man, according to Aquinas, because many men, as a matter of observed fact, do not believe in God.[16] Man does, however, have a confused knowledge of God inasmuch as man desires that perfect happiness which can only be discovered in God.[17] Additionally, man infers, by way of sensory perception, a general, albeit imperfect notion of a first cause by which other things come to exist. Aquinas famously offered five arguments to prove the point that God can be inferred as the general cause of the created order. Central to each of these arguments is the premise that every effect contains something of its cause:

> Yet from every effect the existence of the cause can be clearly demonstrated, and so we can demonstrate the existence of God from His effects, though from them we cannot perfectly know God as He is in His essence.[18]

Having demonstrated, then, how far philosophy can carry us unto a general, albeit deficient knowledge of God as first cause, Aquinas quickly moves on to theology, the science which deals specifically with God's divine revelation.

The doctrine of simplicity is a major cornerstone of Aquinas' theology. As the contemporary Christian philosopher, Alvin Plantinga, points out, "When Thomas Aquinas embarks on the task of characterizing God's attributes, simplicity is the first item on his list."[19]

The doctrine of simplicity is seemingly given a place of such prominence because it is viewed as determining, to some extent at least,

---

15 Aquinas, *Summa Theologica*, 1.1.10.

16 Aquinas, *Summa Theologica*, 1.2.1.

17 Aquinas, *Summa Theologica*, 1.2.1.

18 Aquinas, *Summa Theologica*, 1.2.2.

19 Plantinga, *Nature*, 28.

the character of all of God's other attributes. Simplicity entails that all of God's attributes are identical to God himself and thus, identical to one another. Aquinas subordinates all of God's attributes to the doctrine of simplicity, both logically and, in the context of his *Summa Theologica*, chronologically.

If I may interject for a moment, given that theology is, according to Aquinas, the science that deals with the divine revelation, it seems a curious—if not haphazard—procedure to subordinate all of those attributes of God which are explicitly mentioned in Scripture to the doctrines of simplicity, which is nowhere explicitly mentioned in Scripture.

According to Aquinas, humans possess *being* as something given to them by God, but God alone is identical to his being.[20] Since God is identical to his own essence and nature, "therefore, it is clear that God is in no way composite, but is altogether simple."[21] Aquinas seems to appeal to the doctrine of simplicity to ward against the possibility of having anything outside of God's control. If "existence," for example, is something that is not identical to God himself, then seemingly it could stand as an outside, third party. Presumably God would have to acquire his existence from some outside source: "Therefore that thing whose being differs from its essence must have its being caused by another."[22] The doctrine of simplicity guarantees that God did not acquire his existence from some external source, for simplicity requires that God *is* his own existence. Aquinas' sentiment is that if God is identical to his own existence, then obviously we need look no further than God himself for the source of God's existence, for "God" and "Existence" are one and the same. In Aquinas' language, the two are convertible terms. Simplicity thus helps Aquinas avoid an infinite regress of existence, whereby even God himself would seemingly require a source for

20 Aquinas, *Summa Theologica*, 1.3.4.

21 Aquinas, *Summa Theologica*, 1.3.7.

22 Aquinas, *Summa Theologica*, 1.3.4.

his existence. For Aquinas, in summary, every being derives their being from some other being, with the exception of God, who is being itself.

If I may speak frankly, I don't think this sort of argument carries very much weight anymore. I think that modern man, by and large, is suspicious of the strong realism inherent to the argument. I think that we recognize much more clearly that "existence" is not a concrete quality that creatures possess, but is something more along the lines of an abstract assessment. To continue with this slight detour, Plato had entertained the idea—silly to modern man—that every word must refer to some concrete entity. Even relational terms such as "smallness" and "actuality" were spoken of as divine Forms that probably exist in outer space somewhere. This type of strong realism attempted to turn every verb, adjective, and adverb into a proper noun. Abstract concepts were re-imagined as concrete objects.

The modern term for re-imagining an intramental concept (i.e., a concept inside of the mind) as a concrete, extramental entity in the outside world is "reification." In connection with Christian Theology, that seems to me a very important term to remember. "Smallness," for example, is obviously an abstract mental evaluation of one object's size (or significance) relative to some other object. It is a term of relative comparison. To imagine that there is some concrete object in another realm called "smallness" which all other small things must "participate" in is clearly an intellectual mistake, and not a small one.

Obviously, we have to carefully distinguish between concrete things that exist in the outside world and abstract ideas that exist only inside the mind. Admittedly, it's not always easy to do so; the two blend seamlessly in human experience. It seems, at times, a profoundly daunting labyrinth to navigate. It seems plain enough, however, that ancient man had a bad habit of turning concepts into concrete beings. Every concept became a god in the ancient world. Ancient man had his god of war, his god of romance, his god of fertility, his god of retribution, and so on. When Jesus said that we cannot serve both God and Mammon (Matthew 6:24), he seems to have been referencing a Chaldean god of money. Money had been reimagined as a personal being. Obviously, ancient man had a bad habit of reifying concepts into concrete beings. I would argue that Plato's Forms represent a similar sort of intellectual mistake.

The German philosopher, Immanuel Kant (1724–1804), famously argued that existence is not a predicate, and I think that Kant was right on this point. To say that "I exist" is not to say that I possess some concrete quality "existence" like I concretely possess arms and legs and eyeballs. Rather, to say that "I exist" is to make a *conceptual evaluation* of the fact that I am here.

"Existence" is no more a concrete object than "non-existence." If I describe something as "non-existent," I am not saying that there is some being that possesses the concrete quality "non-existence." Rather, I am simply saying that the thing in question is not a thing at all; rather, it's a *no-thing*. To say that unicorns, for example, don't exist is to say that some concept in my mind doesn't have any actual corollary in the world outside of the mind. The intramental concept has no extramental being.

Likewise, to say that "I exist" is not to say that I possess some concrete quality "existence." Rather, it means that I am a *thing* and not a *no-thing*. "Existence" is an evaluative concept in the mind and not a proper attribute or predicate. "Existence" is purely abstract and conceptual. Existence is not a thing, but an idea.

It should be kept in mind, in this connection, that Aristotle, no less than Plato, accepted the literal, concrete existence of the Forms. To be sure, Aristotle rejected the need to posit a divine realm in which the Forms have an independent existence "apart" from matter,[23] but he nevertheless believed that the Forms really existed, concretely, within physical objects. Though they differ on many points, both Plato and

23 Aristotle, *Metaphysics*, 991b[0], 509.

Aristotle were realists about the Forms. The paragraph to follow will give the reader a bit of the flavor of Aristotle's view.

Following Aristotle, Aquinas taught that any particular individual is the combination of a bit of matter in conjunction with a realist Form. Aquinas said that "it is manifest that everything actually existing possesses a form, and thus its matter is determined by form."[24] For Aquinas, any particular individual is a bit of prime matter (conceived as the generic, formless play-dough of the universe) in conjunction with a distinct Form. Any particular man is a particular bit of matter in conjunction with the human Form. Any particular horse is a bit of matter in conjunction with the horse Form. And so on. Forms were thus imagined to be the mold or underlying framework of individual things. Every individual thing was imagined to contain a Form that determined it to be precisely what it was. We recognize all humans *as human* precisely because each member of the class is in possession of the human Form. The human Form is imagined to be every bit as concretely real as the individual human.

Aquinas likewise had a strongly realist understanding of "existence" and "being." Like Dionysius, he imagined that God is identical to existence and being, as such, and that God generously extends these concrete predicates to man. Aquinas reminds us of Plato when he says, "Therefore, all beings apart from God are not their own being, but are beings by participation."[25] So God, as original concrete *being* and original concrete *existence* extends being and existence to man such that man participates in being and existence alongside God.

Where Aquinas thought of "existence" as a concrete quality or object (not entirely unlike a Platonic Form), simplicity would guarantee that "existence" is identical to God, and not something he acquired from some outside source. Yet if "existence" is, as I have suggested, not a concrete object or quality at all, but something more along the

24 Aquinas, *Summa Theologica*, 1.7.2.

25 Aquinas, *Summa Theologica*, 1.44.1.

lines of an abstract, mental evaluation, then the problem perceived by Aquinas evaporates like the morning mist and the entire argument is invalidated. For it is nonsensical to ask where God obtains the concrete quality "existence" from if "existence" is not a concrete quality to begin with. Aquinas was clearly thinking in terms of a strong realism like that of Plato and therein lies the problem. He failed to recognize that "existence" and "being" are abstract concepts, and not concrete things.

Inevitably, the doctrine of simplicity created numerous epistemological problems for Aquinas. As is well-rehearsed by now, man is unable to think about God in simple terms. According to Aquinas, "we are unable to understand simple self-subsisting forms as they really are, but understand them after the mode of composite things having forms in matter."[26] Since we cannot think about the simple God in simple terms, we discover an unfortunate disconnect between God himself and the human knowledge of God.

The doctrine of simplicity teaches us that when we think about God having various names and various attributes, our conceptions of God *as manifold* are, to that extent, incorrect. Our knowledge of God's attributes has to be constantly qualified by our knowledge of the fact that God does not actually have a plurality of attributes:

> God, however, considered in Himself, is altogether one and simple, yet our intellect knows Him by different conceptions because it cannot see Him as He is in Himself. Nevertheless, although it understands Him under different conceptions, it knows that all its conceptions correspond to one and the same thing absolutely.[27]

Given that mankind thinks in non-simple terms, and given that God is simple, it follows that we can never think about God precisely

26 Aquinas, *Summa Theologica*, 1.13.9.

27 Aquinas, *Summa Theologica*, 1.13.12.

as he is. At the very moment we say that God is simple, we must also concede that we don't know precisely what we mean by it.

For Aquinas, man thinks about God in a way that is not strictly applicable to God, considered in his essence, as God. Man thinks in human terms where God thinks in divine terms, and the two are quite contrary to one another. Man thinks in one "mode" where God thinks in an altogether different mode. This distinction between two "modes" of being—implicit in Clement, Augustine, and Dionysius—becomes explicit for the first time in Aquinas:

> Now, our intellect cannot attain to the absolute simplicity of the divine essence considered in itself, and therefore, our human intellect apprehends and names divine things *according to its own mode*, that is in so far as they are found in sensible things from which its knowledge is derived.[28]

Aquinas thus distinguishes between God as he is known to us and God as he really is, in his own essence. This is, by now, a familiar distinction. Aquinas agreed with Dionysius that we can only describe divine things in the manner of our own comprehension, that is, within our own mode of being. God-in-himself cannot be properly translated into human logic or language, for God is simple, and our logic and language cannot properly express the truth about God in simple terms.

For Aquinas, we know God in a human way, but God is, of course, not human. When we predicate "goodness," "justice," and the like to God we seem to be suggesting that God possesses these qualities as we understand them. Yet we cannot understand them in the divine way but only in the human way. Our knowledge of God is necessarily limited to thinking about God within the human mode, and so God-in-himself is wholly outside of our purview. Given the difficulty, Aquinas repeatedly and consistently insists that we cannot know God, as God, in this life:

---

28 Aquinas, *Summa Theologica*, 1.32.2.

> We cannot know the essence of God in this life, as He really is in Himself; but we know Him according as He is represented in the perfections of creatures; and thus names imposed by us signify Him in that manner only.[29]

Even divine revelation cannot reveal God to us *as simple*, for a written revelation must necessarily reveal God to us page by page, temporally, successively, and by way of a (composite) composition. Here again, we see the importance of Aquinas' idea (borrowed from Dionysius) that God is known by us only through his effects. Our knowledge of God is really a knowledge of God's effects, as found in creatures:

> Now it was shown above that in this life we cannot see the essence of God; but we know God from creatures as their principle, and also by way of excellence and remotion [i.e., apophatic negation]. In this way therefore He can be named by us from creatures, yet not so that the name which signifies Him expresses the divine essence in itself...[30]

All human talk of divine things is necessarily within the human mode. We cannot think about God as God thinks about God, for we do not have divine minds. "Divine things are named by our intellect not as they really are in themselves, for in that way it knows them not, but in a way that belongs to things created."[31] Accordingly, Aquinas affirms the *via negativa* and asserts that we cannot say what God-in-himself really is. We can only say what God-in-himself is not.[32] We have no knowledge of who God-in-himself is:

> When the existence of a thing has been ascertained there remains the further question of the manner of its existence, in

29 Aquinas, *Summa Theologica*, 1.13.2.

30 Aquinas, *Summa Theologica*, 1.13.1.

31 Aquinas, *Summa Theologica*, 1.39.2.

32 Copleston, *History*, V2, 348.

> order that we may know what it is. Now, because *we cannot know what God is, but rather what He is not*, we have no means for considering how God is, but rather how He is not.[33]

Aquinas is not ultimately a skeptic about the knowledge of God, however. His view is that we finally obtain a proper knowledge of God-in-himself in the afterlife by a special act of divine grace and glorification. Aquinas looked forward to a future hope and believed that glorified saints finally come to know God as God:

> God cannot be seen in His essence by a mere human being, *unless he be separated from this mortal life.* The reason is, because, as was said above, the mode of knowledge follows the mode of the nature of the knowing thing. But our soul, *as long as we live in this life*, has its being in corporeal matter; hence naturally it knows only what has a form in matter, or what can be known in this way. Now it is evident that the divine essence cannot be known through the natures of material things. For it was shown above that the knowledge of God by means of any created likeness is not the vision of His essence. *Hence it is impossible for the soul of man in this life to see the essence of God.*[34]

Though it is impossible to know God-in-himself on this side of the grave, in death the saint will see God as he is. Man's grand desire to know God, as God, is man's greatest source of happiness and this desire will not ultimately be frustrated, according to Aquinas. To see God and to understand God, as God, is man's *summum bonum* or supreme good. After death, man shall, in his glorification, be conformed to the image of God. The glorified Christian will, in Aquinas' terminology, be made "deiform."[35]

---

33 Aquinas, *Summa Theologica*, 1.3.preface.

34 Aquinas, *Summa Theologica*, 1.12.11.

35 See Aquinas, *Summa Theologica*, 1.12.5.

Aquinas repeatedly refers to 1 John 3:2 as proof of this future reality. The passage reads, "Beloved, now we are children of God, and it has not appeared as yet what we will be. We know that when He appears, we will be like Him, because we will see Him just as He is." According to Aquinas, the glorified saints are able to see God-in-himself (directly and not through any intermediary likeness)[36] on account of "the divine essence itself united to their intellect."[37] Aquinas meant that since we will be conformed to God, as the children of God, we will finally understand God-in-himself for the first time. He believed that the Christian undergoes an ontological as well as ethical and epistemic transformation upon death.

However, even then we will not know God-in-himself comprehensively.[38] Rather, we will understand him in part, having a view of some of his "boundaries."[39] Aquinas raises a powerful objection to himself at this point: a simple God seemingly could not be known in part, for a simple God has no parts.[40] You cannot know a simple God *partially* without allowing that God has parts and is, therefore, not simple. If the glorified saint only sees this or that aspect of God or this or that boundary, then it follows that God has various, distinct aspects and boundaries. A simple God cannot have aspects or boundaries, however, for these would certainly represent parts of God. In the scheme of divine simplicity, every part of God must be said to be identical to the whole of God. Thus, to see any part of the simple God would necessarily be to see *all* of the simple God. To know the simple God, in other words, we must know him immediately and comprehensively. In his response to this objection, Aquinas merely appeals to the authority of Augustine, and says that we can, in fact, know the simple

---

36 See Aquinas, *Summa Theologica*, 1.12.9.

37 Aquinas, *Summa Theologica*, 1.12.9.

38 See Aquinas, *Summa Theologica*, 1.12.7.

39 Aquinas, *Summa Theologica*, 1.12.7.

40 See Aquinas, *Summa Theologica*, 1.12.7. See objection 2.

God partially. This seems to me a grossly inadequate answer to a very devastating objection. Since man would seemingly have to become simple to know the simple, time-less to know the time-less, consistency would seem to favor a pantheism like that of Plotinus.

According to Aquinas, revelation cannot describe God-in-himself as he actually is, but speaks instead in metaphors and analogies. The divine names given to God in Scripture, for example, "fail to express His mode of being, since our intellect does not know Him in this life as He is."[41] Scripture cannot possibly speak in divine terms for our minds exist on a lower plane of existence, in a lower mode. The divine names in the Bible "do not properly and strictly apply to God, for their mode of signification applies to creatures."[42] None of our knowledge of God strictly applies to God-in-himself. Such knowledge is reserved for the hereafter.

Though Aquinas offers us hope of obtaining some knowledge of God-in-himself in the afterlife, he seems to offer quite a bleak picture of the Christian knowledge of God in this life. Our knowledge of God at this time is, according to Aquinas, merely a knowledge of God's effects in his creatures. If we say, for example, that "God is good" what we are really saying is that goodness, as humanly understood, is a predicate of God, inasmuch as God is humanly understood. Yet the human understanding of God is not a simple understanding of God, and therefore the human understanding of God is strictly inapplicable to God himself. The simple God does not have various predicates like we do and so nothing we say about God is said *properly* of God. To say that "God is good" is to suggest that "God" and "goodness" are not identical, but this is false, according to Aquinas, for "God" and "goodness" are convertible terms in a manner that we cannot really even begin to come to grips with intellectually. All of our predications about God are unreal in a sense, though Aquinas insists that they are not false.[43]

41 Aquinas, *Summa Theologica*, 1.13.1.

42 Aquinas, *Summa Theologica*, 1.13.3.

43 See Copleston, *History*, V2, 361.

Unsurprisingly, Aquinas also described God as time-less. "Whatever is wholly immutable can have no succession."[44] Eternity is simple and has no parts.[45] God's eternity is "simultaneously whole" such that the idea of time must be removed.[46] Since eternity "is always the same, there is no before and after."[47] Aquinas tells us that it is not technically correct to say that God is eternal for simplicity requires that God is identical with his eternity. Better to say God is eternity than that God is eternal.[48] Aquinas also insists that God's time-less eternity "includes all times."[49] Eternity is the "simultaneous whole" of all time.[50] God's time-less eternity is comprehensive of human time:

> ...since eternity is without succession, comprehending all time, the present glance of God extends over all time, and to all things which exist in any time, as to subjects present to Him.[51]

Aquinas seems to overlook the fact that a "present glance" presupposes time inasmuch as the "present" is still a time referent and inasmuch as every "glance" inevitably takes time to carry out. Aquinas has here lapsed into thinking about God in temporal terms, as we all inevitably must.

Aquinas said that since God is above time, he has a unique vantage upon time. He likened God's knowledge of time to a man who stands atop a tall building and surveys the street below. According to Aquinas, "he who sees the whole road from a height sees at once all travelling by

---

44 Aquinas, *Summa Theologica*, 1.10.1.
45 Aquinas, *Summa Theologica*, 1.10.1.
46 Aquinas, *Summa Theologica*, 1.10.1.
47 Aquinas, *Summa Theologica*, 1.10.1.
48 See Copleston, *History*, V2, 349.
49 Aquinas, *Summa Theologica*, 1.10.2.
50 Aquinas, *Summa Theologica*, 1.14.13.
51 Aquinas, *Summa Theologica*, 1.14.9.

the way."[52] Of course, even with a perfect vantage point, *surveying* the present happenings on the street below still presupposes time.

It also remains unclear how our temporal history could be compatible with God's succession-less state of being. Our history contains lots and lots of succession, of course, one event following upon the heels of another. To remove *succession* from our history would seemingly be to remove an essential element of it. Our history would become quite unlike the history we know if we removed all the succession inherent to it. The same may be said of terms such as "before" and "after." Aquinas insists that God has no befores or afters. Yet, obviously, our history has many of them. How then could the two ever be made compatible? Our history of succession would seemingly be strictly incompatible with God's succession-less history. God's simple time, so to speak, would be antithetical to our manifold time.

Aquinas acknowledged that Scripture speaks of God as though he bears a direct relationship to time, but said that this is purely anthropomorphic.[53] This is merely God presented as if he were a creature. A simple God must be identical to his own situation as well as his own actions.[54] As with time, God also has a unique relationship to space. He does not occupy space in the same manner we do, but rather his "whole self is everywhere."[55]

As in Augustine, angels stand midway between time and God's time-less eternity.[56] Aquinas refers to this state of being as aeviternity. "Aeviternity is more simple than time, and is nearer to eternity."[57]

---

52 Aquinas, *Summa Theologica*, 1.14.13.

53 Aquinas, *Summa Theologica*, 1.10.1.

54 Aquinas seems to indicate that God is identical to his own actions in 1.13.7, when he says "...the action of God, which is His essence." Simplicity seems to require as much. Yet if God is identical to his act of creation, for instance, pantheism seems to follow.

55 Aquinas, *Summa Theologica*, 1.8.4.

56 Aquinas, *Summa Theologica*, 1.10.5.

57 Aquinas, *Summa Theologica*, 1.10.6.

Aquinas' notion of one thing being "more simple" than another seems nonsensical, however, for simplicity, by definition, is a reductive all-or-nothing concept. Either a thing has internal distinctions or it doesn't. Aquinas himself said that "what is simple is undivided, both actually and potentially."[58] To be simple is to be indivisible in every conceivable sense. Thus you cannot have "more" or "less" of simplicity. It's clearly nonsense to talk about a hierarchy of being where various species possess different degrees of being and simplicity.

Once again without surprise, Aquinas says that God is impassible. God, on this account, experiences no emotions:

> Anger and the like are attributed to God on account of a likeness of effect. Thus, because to punish is properly the act of an angry man, God's punishment is metaphorically spoken of as His anger.[59]

The emotions displayed by God in Scripture are purely metaphorical for Aquinas. In describing these emotions as metaphorical, Aquinas really only seems to have meant that we read emotions into God because we are emotional creatures.

As in Augustine, God is immutable or absolutely unchanging for Aquinas. Accordingly, God cannot bear a new relationship to man for God never has any new relationships. "He cannot acquire anything new, nor extend Himself to anything to which He was not extended previously."[60] When God in Scripture is said to "draw near" us and the like, "These things are said of God in Scripture metaphorically. For as the sun is said to enter a house or to go out according as its rays reach the house, so God is said to approach to us or to recede from us when we receive the influx of His goodness, or fall away from Him."[61] Since

58 Aquinas, *Summa Theologica*, 1.11.1.

59 Aquinas, *Summa Theologica*, 1.3.2. See the reply to Objection 2.

60 Aquinas, *Summa Theologica*, 1.9.1.

61 Aquinas, *Summa Theologica*, 1.9.1.

God does not change in any sense of the word, seemingly God cannot personally and dynamically relate to me now any more than he related to me before I was born.

Though Scripture ascribes a great diversity of qualities, traits, and names to God, "it must be ascribed to the diversity which lies in the way our intellect receives, and not to any diversity in reality."[62] The diverse attributes of God found in Scripture must be understood as metaphorical and accommodative inasmuch as God is simple and does not have a diversity of attributes and qualities. Seemingly, the God of Scripture is quite unlike the God that actually exists as God.

Borrowing a distinction from Aristotle, Aquinas said that God is pure actuality. "Actuality" is defined as what a being *actually is*, which is contrasted with "potency," which is a being's potential to be or do something other than what they are presently being or doing. I am *actually* a forty-three-year-old man trying to write a book. I can potentially go to the store, or potentially go to bed. I can potentially become an elderly man or a dead man. Since God is immutable or unchanging in the strictest sense, he is always the same as himself and he is always doing precisely what he always has been doing. He cannot *be* or *do* or *experience* anything new, for that would implicate God in change.

Aristotle's act/potency distinction closely parallels Plato's being/becoming distinction. God is said to be *pure actuality* and *pure being*. He has no potency and no becoming. Aristotle taught that since the Prime Mover (i.e., God) is pure, unchangeable actuality, he moves the Cosmos not by way of willful choice but more in the manner that a stationary magnet might naturally move another object which comes near it. The Prime Mover is absolutely static, stationary, and immutable, though other objects are moved around it. Aristotle would have certainly rejected the Christian conception that God created the

62 Aquinas, *Summa Theologica*, 1.3.3.

world by fiat, that is, by a free act of will, for that would most certainly involve God in potentiality and in change.

Still today, classical theists drone on about how God is pure actuality with no potency and seem blind to the fact that they have thereby defined God as im-potent and powerless. If God has no potency, he certainly cannot *potentially* create a world like this one! Nor can he potentially save sinners! If God is pure actuality, then he cannot potentially do anything at all! To say that God is pure actuality with no potency is to make God altogether impotent to effect change in any sort of dynamic sense. Despite the best of intentions, this seems more insulting than complimentary. Though it sounds quite sophisticated to say that God is "pure being" and "pure actuality," it's obvious that the great majority of theologians who parrot these pagan expressions haven't really thought through their import.

In the thought of Aquinas (as in that of Dionysius), just as man faces the impossibility of trying to attain a knowledge of God-in-himself in this life, so too God seems to face a similar difficulty. Just as the human range of vision is limited to the manifold and temporal, so too God's range of vision is seemingly limited to his simple and timeless point of view. Whatever God sees, he sees as simple:

> So we say that God sees Himself in Himself, because He sees Himself through His essence; and He sees other things not in themselves, but in Himself, because His essence contains the likeness of things other than Himself.[63]

Whereas human reasoning is discursive, that is, piece by piece, and little by little, God is not capable of reasoning discursively.[64] Although God knows the complexity of the world exhaustively, he sees it only through himself and his own simplicity. Aquinas repeats the rule that

63 Aquinas, *Summa Theologica*, 1.14.4.

64 Aquinas, *Summa Theologica*, 1.14.7.

"what is outside Himself He does not see except in Himself."[65] Thus, God cannot know me as I am—as a manifold and complex thing—rather, I am interpreted by God through the lens of God's simplicity: "God knows things other than Himself according as they are in Himself."[66]

This seems problematic because it implies that God is incapable of understanding precisely how humans think. God knows all of our thoughts, of course, for Aquinas, but not in the precise manner that we do. We know our thoughts in a manifold and temporal manner, but not so with God. In such a case, it seems to me, it would not be true to say that God knows all that can be known. Obviously, God is not omniscient if he doesn't know how human reasoning works *as humans know it.* If God cannot know something in the way that I know it, then obviously he does not know all that can be known.

To the present author, it seems important to distinguish between discursive learning and discursive reasoning. Obviously, humans learn things little by little over the span of our lives. We take in information through a long, step-by-step process. By contrast, God knows all things and has always known all things. He cannot learn anything new, and, in fact, he has never learned anything at all, for he always knew all that could be known. Clearly, God is unlike man in this regard. God does not and cannot *learn* discursively.

Even so, God can *reason* discursively, or else he is not all-knowing. God knows all of the facts of mathematics, for example, and he is conscious of all of those facts all of the time. God knows, for example, that 1+1=2. Yet the arithmetical equation 1+1=2 is a discursive fact. I arrive at the 2 by adding the 1 to the 1. That's how it works. Understanding the equation 1+1=2 necessitates the understanding of a sequence. It necessitates a logical, discursive development. Discursivity

65 Aquinas, *Summa Theologica*, 1.14.5.

66 Aquinas, *Summa Theologica*, 1.14.6.

is inherent to mathematics, considered as a system (or group of systems) with an inherent, internal development.

The equation 1+1=2 is a discursive fact; it implies movement and development. I have to understand what "1" means and what "2" means and what the "+" sign and the "=" sign means. I have to run through the sequence. Yet a simple God would seemingly be unable to walk through this type of successive operation. A simple God could not know this particular non-simple fact (at least not in the same way that I do), and would, therefore, not be omniscient.

Likewise, a time-less God would seemingly struggle to understand how 1+1=2 works because the sequence itself inevitably takes time to carry out. A time-less God could seemingly not know this sequential fact, as sequential, and thus would not be omniscient.

Seemingly, a simple God could not understand manifold facts *as manifold, and* a time-less God could not know the facts of time *as temporal.* Not only could man not know God-in-himself, but neither could God know man-in-himself. God and man would each be stuck in their respective caves with no point of epistemological contact.

Aquinas noted that many of the biblical names of God such as "Creator" and "Savior" seem to imply temporality, where the act of creating and the act of saving are naturally imagined as temporal operations. Normally, we imagine that God stepped into time in order to create the temporal world and in order to secure the temporal redemption of mankind. Aquinas notes that while it is appropriate to apply such terms to God, it must be understood that the relations imagined are really from the human perspective and are strictly inapplicable to God-in-himself. Though we relate temporally to God, God cannot relate temporally to us, for God is strictly immutable and cannot bear new relations:

> Since therefore God is outside the whole order of creation, and all creatures are ordered to Him, and not conversely, it is manifest that creatures are really related to God Himself; in God however *there is no real relation to creatures,* but a

> relation according to reason only, in so far as creatures are referred to Him.[67]

So while God is a Savior and Creator from the human perspective, we should not imagine that God entered into time or performed some new action when he created the world or redeemed mankind. A timeless and immutable God cannot do anything new. He must always *be* precisely what he has always been and must always *do* precisely what he has always done. Aquinas said that terms such as Savior and Creator do not refer to the essence of God, either directly or indirectly.[68] Even creation and redemption are static, fixed realities for God. God knows variable things in his own, unique, invariable way. "Now created things are in God in an invariable manner, while they exist variably in themselves."[69] Presumably, from God's succession-less point of view, there was never a time when creation was not.

If I may again interject, at a practical level, this view seems quite demoralizing. When I pray to God, I assume that God is actively listening to my temporal and non-simple prayers and actively communing with me in responsive fellowship. Simpleton that I am, if I believed that God was not presently engaged with me when I pray, sitting right here beside me in time, as it were, I think I would find it difficult to justify prayer in the first place. Here we see classical theism and relational theism in sharp contrast, where the classical theist (when consistent) denies that God relates dynamically to man, and the relational theist adamantly affirms that God has a dynamic, responsive, temporal relationship with every human soul.

Aquinas said that we discover an "analogical" knowledge of God in divine revelation.[70] Again we find the importance of Aquinas' doctrine

67 Aquinas, *Summa Theologica*, 1.13.7.

68 Aquinas, *Summa Theologica*, 1.13.7.

69 Aquinas, *Summa Theologica*, 1.14.15.

70 Aquinas, *Summa Theologica*, 1.13.5.

that God is known through his effects. What he meant is that revelation gives us analogies about God, by likening God to the created order. God is likened to his effects in creation. Though it is perfectly appropriate to say, for example, that "God is good," it is to be understood that God does not possess a goodness like that goodness known to us. To say "God is good" is effectively describing God as a creature by saying that God has goodness in the creaturely, human sense of the word. It is perfectly appropriate, of course, to say that "God is good" but we should nevertheless recognize that we are not saying it *properly* of God-in-himself. For Aquinas, all of our talk about God contains this inherent limitation, for all human talk falls within the boundaries of the human mode of being, where God-in-himself is wholly outside the human mode, both ontologically and epistemologically. We never speak of God *properly*; we only speak of God in human metaphors, as if God were human.

Analogical knowledge is imagined to be a midpoint between univocal knowledge and equivocal knowledge. This, of course, requires further definitions. Univocal knowledge is conceived of as an identical (or, at least, similar) knowledge, as when one human addresses another in terms that both understand in approximately the same sense, and information is accurately communicated. The thoughts of one person become the thoughts of another person via verbal or written communication. (It may be helpful to know that uni-vocal, according to its etymology, means "one voice".)

Equivocal knowledge is the opposite, as when two people speak different languages and so at least some information is lost in translation. Two people speaking the same language may likewise define their terms differently such that the two end up speaking past one another to some extent. In either case, the exchange of information is at least partially unsuccessful. As Aquinas' described it:

> Univocal terms mean absolutely the same thing, but equivocal terms absolutely different things; but in analogical terms

> a word taken in one signification must be placed in the definition of the same word taken in other senses...[71]

Univocal communication is, roughly, accurate communication within the same mode of being and equivocal communication would be a case where communication had failed to some extent. Since, according to Aquinas, no human words can appropriately apply to God-in-himself, man possesses no univocal knowledge of God: "I answer that, univocal predication is impossible between God and creatures."[72] For Aquinas, we possess a true knowledge of God, but it is a true knowledge that consists entirely of creaturely metaphors and analogies. Our knowledge of God is really only a knowledge of God's effects, as found in creatures.

Several of Aquinas' successors, such as Duns Scotus (c. 1265–1308) and William of Ockham (1287-1347), took issue with Aquinas' notion of analogical knowledge because it is unclear what exactly the positive content of analogical predication is. The term "analogical" refers, of course, to an analogy. An analogy presents a familiar thing in a more inventive, unfamiliar way. We say, for example, that someone is as "stubborn as a mule." Such comparisons can, of course, be of many different types. Yet for any analogy to hold true, there must be some real point of univocal comparison. An analogy that doesn't make a real, proper comparison would certainly fail as an analogy.

Any given analogy can only be successful if there is genuine overlap between the two objects or ideas being compared (e.g., the person and the mule have a similar sort of stubbornness). An analogy or metaphor devoid of any univocal, common core would fail as an analogy or metaphor, for no information would be communicated.

As a rule of formal logic in the medieval era, whenever the logician came across an analogy, it was his job to convert the analogy into

71 Aquinas, *Summa Theologica*, 1.13.10.

72 Aquinas, *Summa Theologica*, 1.13.5.

an ordinary proposition so as to analyze the validity of the point being made. To do that, the logician would identify the univocal element (i.e., the point of real, proper comparison) in the analogy. Because of their extensive knowledge of formal logic, Scotus and Ockham were acutely aware that it is meaningless to say our knowledge of God is *analogical* if you cannot tell us what part of the analogy represents God *as he is*.

If our knowledge of God is really midway between knowing God precisely as he is (purely univocally) and knowing nothing of God whatsoever (purely equivocally), we must know which part of the analogy teaches us truth about God, where the "truth" in question is the univocal core of the analogy. If no univocal truth is communicated in the analogy, then the analogy has failed as an analogy, and Aquinas' conception of "analogical" knowledge is discovered to be vacuous.

In other words, if the analogies in Scripture do not communicate truths about God-in-himself to us, as he is in himself, then they have failed as analogies. If scriptural analogies do not provide us with accurate and proper information about God-in-himself, what, then, are they really analogies of? Seemingly, they are only analogies about man and about the human mode of being. The analogy is really only an analogy about ourselves, but, in that case, it is not really an analogy *about God* at all.

In Aquinas' Neoplatonic scheme, whatever analogies we possess about God in Scripture do not and cannot communicate anything about that which is *properly divine*. Do we actually possess useful analogies that clearly communicate to us what time-lessness or simplicity are like? Of course not. Thus, the word "analogical" seems little more than a cryptic piece of sophistry used to avoid the embarrassing admission that we don't know anything whatsoever about God.

This criticism of Scotus and Ockham seems to me definitive; Aquinas' view is indefensible. While he certainly wanted to know information about God, an implicit Platonism prevented access. He did not discover a way beyond the Platonic Divorce that separates man from God. God and man have been defined as dualistic opposites. God and man have mutually exclusive modes of being. Ultimately, Scripture reveals nothing about God, as God, according to Aquinas, for Scripture speaks exclusively in human terms, and exclusively in the human mode.

Aquinas fully embraced the structure of Platonic metaphysic. Man is divorced from God just as God is divorced from man. We are "united to Him as to one unknown [!]."[73] Man is out of God's reach just as surely as God is out of man's reach. The notion that we will be at least partially translated into the divine mode of being after death is highly problematic. It's difficult to see how pantheism could be avoided.

We need to be very clear that God *as he is* (or God-in-himself, or God in his essence) is just God himself, that is, the God that actually exists as God. To say that we don't know God *as he is* is precisely the same as saying we don't know the first thing about God, and that God is not—and cannot be—discovered in the Bible. It seems that we must return again to Socrates and ask, why should we listen to what Aquinas has to say about God when, by his own account, he knows nothing at all about God, as God?

An encyclical letter from Pope Leo XIII in 1879 and the Code of Canon Law in 1917 made Aquinas the official theologian of the Roman Church. Rome is henceforth forever bound to teach the doctrines of Neoplatonism as supposedly Christianized by Aquinas. As Inge noted, "As long as St. Thomas Aquinas is the norm of scientific orthodoxy, the philosophy of the Church must remain predominantly Neoplatonic."[74] In true, purgatorial fashion, Rome has consigned itself to be forever stuck in the Dark Ages in all matters theological.

---

73 Aquinas, *Summa Theologica*, 1.12.13.

74 Inge, *Plotinus*, 15.

9

Stephen Charnock

NO single work has greater claim to being the modern classic on the doctrine of God than Stephen Charnock's *Discourses upon the Existence and Attributes of God.* Originally delivered as a series of sermons to his church congregation, the lectures were published posthumously in two large volumes. The work is both warm and scholarly. The second discourse, in particular, is one of the most compelling and insightful in all of Christian literature. Charnock will here serve us well as a mature voice of Reformational thought. His Protestant orthodoxy is beyond reproach.

Stephen Charnock (1628–1680) was an English Puritan and Presbyterian clergyman. His life seems to have been, for the most part, uneventful, consumed by the quiet pursuits of reading, writing, and preparing his Sunday sermon. Though he cannot match the likes of Augustine and Aquinas for philosophical acumen, he excels both of them in careful biblical exegesis, knowledge of the original biblical languages, and ardent practical application of Scriptural truth.

Some contrasts with past thought quickly become apparent. The Scholastic synthesis entailed the systematic harmonization of Scripture, Plato, Aristotle, Augustine, Dionysius, etc. Charnock, by contrast, in conformity with the Protestant principle of *Sola Scriptura*, subordinates all other authority to the unique authority of Scripture as God's written self-revelation. Careful biblical exegesis becomes the all-important focal point; all else is peripheral. Each lengthy chapter is, in fact, an exposition of a key Scriptural text on the specific attribute of God under investigation.

We also find a much stronger emphasis on the doctrine that man is created in the image of God. Augustine and Aquinas had undoubtedly affirmed this biblical teaching, but the major thrust of their thought seemed to head in the opposite direction. Past philosophers had, for the most part, argued for a strict apophatic contrast between God and man. Aquinas, for example, said that while man is something like God (as a creation of God), by contrast, God is nothing like man.[1]

For Charnock, the doctrine that man is made in the image of God seemed, on the contrary, to make God and man similar in a variety of important respects. He often seems to appeal to the doctrine as suggestive of the fact that God and man bear certain native similarities. This seems to push his thought, in some instances at least, in a direction that seemed quite contrary to that of the past.

Let me be clear, however: Charnock was most definitely a classical theist. He was very clearly committed to upholding the traditional view of God that says that God is time-less, immutable, simple, and impassible. He argued, much as I have done, that the doctrines of classical theism inevitably come as a package deal. Simplicity implies immutability: "God were not the most simple being if he were not immutable…Mutability is absolutely inconsistent with simplicity…"[2] Likewise God's time-lessness and immutability seem to suppose one another: "God were not eternal if he were mutable."[3] He frequently cites Augustine and Aquinas to this end.

---

1 See Aquinas, *Summa Theologica*, 1.4.3.

2 Charnock, *Attributes*, 1.333.

3 Charnock, *Attributes*, 1.333.

Yet, overall, Charnock is much less consistent than Augustine and Aquinas. At every turn, he seems to attempt to merge the classical view with a much more practical, pastoral, everyday outlook. It is not always easy to reconcile the academic Charnock with the pastoral Charnock, where the academic clings to the old, rigorous classical theism, and the plain-speaking pastor seems much more inclined to accept a literal interpretation of Scripture's portrayal of God. We shall take the various topics, for the most part, in the order that the author presented them.

According to Charnock, God is eternal and God's eternity is defined as a unique state which encompasses all of human time:

> Eternity is a perpetual duration, which hath neither beginning nor end; time hath both. Those things we say are in time that have beginning, grow up by degrees, have succession of parts; eternity is contrary to time, and is therefore a permanent and immutable state; a perfect possession of life without any variation; it comprehends in itself all years, all ages, all periods of ages; it never begins; it endures after every duration of time, and never ceaseth; it doth as much outrun time, as it went before the beginning of it: time supposeth something before it; but there can be nothing before eternity; it were not then eternity. Time hath a continual succession; the former time passeth away and another succeeds: the last year is not this year, nor this year the next. We must conceive of eternity contrary to the notion of time; as the nature of time consists in the succession of parts, so the nature of eternity in an infinite immutable duration. Eternity and time differ as the sea and rivers; the sea never changes place, and is always one water; but the rivers glide along, and are swallowed up in the sea; so is time by eternity.[4]

4 Charnock, *Attributes*, 1.279-280.

This passage is quite challenging for it seems, superficially at least, to suggest two contrary things. On the one hand, God's eternity is described as a "perpetual duration" which seems to imply that it is a perpetual, endless extent of time. A time-less "duration" would seemingly be a contradiction in terms. Charnock also said that God's eternity encompasses and comprehends all human time within itself which, at first glance at least, seems to imply that human time runs parallel to and concurrent with the divine eternity.

Yet Charnock's overall intent is clear. He insists that God's eternity is "contrary to the notion of time," a state without "succession of parts." Eternity is simple, immutably unchanging, and altogether invariable. Time is swallowed by eternity as the rushing rivers of time run into the unchanging ocean of eternity. Yet it seems a difficult question, to say the least, how could a state without succession or parts comprehend human time, filled to the brim, as it is, with succession and parts?

Charnock tries to settle the difficulty, in one place, by appealing to a popular metaphor:

> There is no succession in God. God is without succession or change… As he hath his whole essence undivided in every place, as well as in an immense space, so he hath all his being in one moment of time, as well as in infinite intervals of time. Some illustrate the difference between eternity and time by the similitude of a tree, or a rock standing upon the side of a river, or shore of the sea; the tree stands always the same and unmoved, while the waters of the river glide along at the foot. The flux is in the river, but the tree acquires nothing but a diverse respect and relation of presence to the various parts of the river as they flow. The waters of the river press on, and push forward one another, and what the river had this minute, it hath not the same the next. So are all sublunary things in a continual flux. …

> But God is the same, without any succession of parts and of time; of him it may be said, "He is." He is no more now than he was, and he shall be no more hereafter than he is. God possesses a firm and absolute being, always constant to himself. He sees all things sliding under him in a continual variation; he beholds the revolutions in the world without any change of his most glorious and immovable nature. All other things pass from one state to another; from their original, to their eclipse and destruction; but God possesses his being in one indivisible point, having neither beginning, end, nor middle.[5]

The notion that God has all of his being in one moment of time quite clearly suggests the classical view that God sees all time as unchangingly present. Yet the suggestion that God's eternity also encompasses "infinite intervals of time" seems to suggest that God, in some sense at least, also experiences time as time. A time-less "interval" would, once again, seemingly be a contradiction in terms.

Charnock seems to have been attempting to reconcile the classical view that God is time-less with the biblical presentation of God as operative in time. He seemingly wants to reconcile God-in-himself to God-as-revealed, by disallowing the distinction. Yet simply stating that time-lessness and time, as well as simplicity and manifold complexity are hereby reconciled hardly seems a satisfactory reconciliation at a philosophical level.

The illustration of a stationary tree with a river rushing alongside is used to demonstrate how the time-less God—the changeless tree—is consistent with the transient river of human history. As previously indicated, however, the illustration is inadequate because not only does the racing of the river presuppose time, but God's *observation* of "all things sliding under him in a continual variation" also presupposes time. It

5 Charnock, *Attributes*, 1.284.

takes time, of course, to examine or observe the rushing of a river. The rushing of the river assumes succession, as does God's beholding all "the revolutions in the world," but Charnock insists that God does not experience succession. Thus, I would submit, once again, that the illustration is inadequate, for it covertly sneaks time into the illustration of how God can oversee the temporal world without time.

A time-less state is literally unimaginable. Humanly speaking, the very act of thinking itself presupposes time. Obviously, no particularly human thought can successfully subtract out the temporal character of the human thought process. It seems to me that Kant was not wrong in insisting that all of our thoughts must inevitably presuppose time.[6] We literally cannot imagine a situation without time. The moment we say that God is time-less, we must also allow that we don't really know what we mean by it.

Charnock seems to fluctuate indecisively between two poles. Oftentimes, he presents God as thinking about time in much the same manner that we do:

> Everything which is the object of God's knowledge without himself was once only future. There was a moment when nothing was in being but himself: he knew nothing actually past, because nothing was past; nothing actually present, because nothing had any existence but himself; therefore only what was future. And why not everything that is future now, as well as only what was future and to come to pass just at the beginning of the creation? God indeed knows everything as present, but the things themselves known by him were not present, but future; the whole creation was once future, or else it was from eternity; if it begun in time, it was once future in itself, else it could never have begun to be.[7]

---

6 One need not be an Idealist to accept the general proposition.

7 Charnock, *Attributes*, 1.431.

Though Charnock insists that God knows everything as present, he seems to also present God as aware of the fact that, at one point in time, nothing existed except himself and everything was future. Superficially at least, this seems a contradiction. For if everything is present to God, then obviously nothing is ever past or future to God. Charnock does little to relieve the tension between these propositions. All is present for God, yet God knows the past as past and the future as future:

> Since God knows time, he knows all things as they are in time; he doth not know all things to be at once, though he knows at once what is, has been, and will be. All things are past, present, and to come, in regard of their existence; but there is not past, present, and to come, in regard of God's knowledge of them, because he sees and knows not by any other, but by himself; he is his own light by which he sees, his own glass wherein he sees; beholding himself, he beholds all things.[8]

Where Augustine and Aquinas seemed to concede that God could not know the past as past or the future as future in his state of eternal presence, Charnock here insisted that God sees the past as past and future as future despite existing in an eternally present state. Once again, he seemed to be trying to reconcile the biblical presentation of God acting freely within time with the classical conception of God as time-less, yet without providing any real logical justification for doing so. Charnock does well to defend God's omniscience, of course, but his view does not seem satisfying at an intellectual level, for he offers no explanation as to how God could see all things as present, while also seeing some things as past and some things as future.

In other places, Charnock more consistently asserts the classical view that God understands time in his own unique, time-less way. The influence of Aquinas is quite evident in some instances:

---

8 Charnock, *Attributes*, 1.285.

> If God be eternal, he knows all things as present. All things are present to him in his eternity; for this is the notion of eternity, to be without succession. If eternity be one indivisible point, and is not diffused into preceding and succeeding parts, then that which is known in it or by it is perceived without any succession, for knowledge is as the substance [i.e., mode] of the person knowing; if that hath various actions and distinct from itself, then it understands things in differences of time as time presents them to view. But, since God's being depends not upon the revolutions of time, so neither does his knowledge; it exceeds all motions of years and days, comprehends infinite spaces of past and future. God considers all things in his eternity in one simple knowledge, as if they were now acted before him…[9]

So God sees all of human history as present before him, as if it was all happening right now. Human history is collapsed into a simple and succession-less scheme. This is, of course, a familiar thought. God is said to see our complex history in light of his own time-less, successionless, simple mode of being. Our history has a past, present, and future, but not so in God's knowledge, for God sees everything as present. Yet what would it mean to know our dynamic history of succession minus the succession inherent to it?

To illustrate the difficulty once again, as I recollect my own individual history, I know that some pieces of my story preceded other pieces. At any given point on my conceptual timeline, I can tell you which parts of the story were earlier and which parts of the story came later. My history consists of a countless number of events, every event being characterized by time and succession. Each event likewise supposed the past, occurred in the present, and preceded the immediate future. If we were to subtract all of the temporality out of my timeline, that version

9 Charnock, *Attributes*, 1.295.

of my timeline would look very little like the original. It wouldn't be a *timeline* at all. It would be a history without succession or movement, but that certainly wouldn't be *my* history.

Charnock insisted, of course, that God's knowledge of our history is perfect, even if translated into his own time-less scheme. Yet it seems obvious that our history translated into simple and time-less terms would be quite unlike itself; it would be a time without plurality, a time without days or years, beginnings, middles, or endings. To know our time in a time-less manner and to know our manifold complexity in a simple manner would be to erase many essential characteristics of the original. To know time *time-lessly* is necessarily to erase those characteristics that make it time. To know complex events *simply* is necessarily to erase all of the distinctions that made them complex events.

If God knows past and future events as present, and has always known them as present, then presumably those characteristics which differentiate them as "past" and "future" would be unknown to him. For us, Jesus died in the past. If God exists in a perpetual present—a state of "eternal now" as we sometimes say—Jesus is still presumably dying in God's eternal present. For us, David and Paul are murderers in the past who made a moral recovery at some later point in time. Presumably for God, the murders of David and Paul are an ever-present reality. Presumably both my birth and my death are always a present reality to God; I haven't been born yet, while simultaneously being long dead.

Simplicity seems to present the same basic obstacle. Take the concept of years, for example. Human history consists of many years, of course. A year is certainly not simple, and a plurality of years is less simple still. So how could God's simple knowledge be compatible with a plurality of years, which is manifestly not simple? You cannot condense our complex history of countless years into a situation that entails no distinctions without destroying the essential character of it. A human history robbed of a plurality of years would hardly be a *human* history.

Charnock could perhaps respond that the apparent contradictions we perceive in these matters is on account of our finite, human limitations and that God's logic is transcendent of our own, such that God can make sense of what we cannot. My response, in turn, would be that if we allow that our rules of logic do not apply to God, then our human theology is a tremendous waste of energy, for we have already established at the beginning, in that case, that we will never discover anything about God as he actually is. All human thought would be strictly inapplicable to God in the event that a different (and unknowable) set of intellectual rules apply to him. Simpleton that I am, I actually hope to obtain some knowledge of *God* when I study theology.

Charnock affirmed that since God is eternal and also simple, it follows that he is identical to his eternity:

> The eternity of God is nothing else but the duration of God; and the duration of God is nothing else but his existence enduring. If eternity were anything distinct from God, and not of the essence of God, then there would be something which was not God, necessary to perfect God.[10]

Charnock said that regenerate man will ultimately join God in eternity. Time will "like a rivulet, fall into the sea of eternity, from whence it sprung."[11] Given that God *is* his eternity, however, to enter God's eternity would seemingly be to enter into God's very being. Of course, this conjures recollections of Plotinus. Charnock did not seem to have recognized the difficulty.

According to Charnock, God cannot change the past into something other than the past, for this would be akin to a contradiction.[12] Seemingly, when God looks from his time-less present down the ever-present corridors of time, he always sees the same thing,

---

10 Charnock, *Attributes*, 1.285.

11 Charnock, *Attributes*, 1.306.

12 Charnock, *Attributes*, 2.29.

immutably. Since the past is always immutably the past, it cannot very well be changed into something other than itself.

This seems to bring into question God's ability to shape the future, however. If God sees the future as immutable and invariable, clearly there is no affecting or shaping anything about it. If the future is present to God, and has always immutably been present, then clearly, the future has already happened. It isn't really "future" at all for God, but present. It was never future for God, for it was always just present. Since it has always been present to God, there is certainly no way he can alter or affect it. It would have just always been a part of his immutable existence. Human history would have always been completed from God's perspective. This makes the actual passage of time altogether irrelevant and unreal. The notion of an eternal present inevitably involves us in the absurdity that, from God's perspective, human history is both complete and, simultaneously, hasn't yet begun. Human history would be both existent and non-existent at the same time and in the same relation, which is, quite plainly, a contradiction.

So Charnock does not seem to be altogether consistent on the issue of time. This is probably to be expected in a work written over many years, published posthumously, and never properly edited by the author. In many instances, he sticks very closely to the view of Aquinas. Yet, in other places, he seems to depart quite widely from it, insisting that God knows time as time and experiences temporal succession.

Charnock seems, in this connection, to quite frequently exploit the ambiguity of the word "eternal." In some contexts, "eternity" seems to mean a unique, time-less, successionless state. In other contexts, "eternity" only seems to indicate an endless duration of time. He says, for example, that our trust in God "should imitate his eternity in its perpetuity."[13] Of course, a time-less state would not have perpetu-

---

13 Charnock, *Attributes*, 1.300.

ity, properly speaking. And we can hardly imitate an eternity that is identical to the being of God himself.

Charnock recognized that the term "eternal" does not appear in the original Hebrew and Greek of Scripture, for it is of later, Latin derivation. He also recognized that the biblical term "everlasting" is not used to speak of a time-less state. According to Charnock, "A thing is said to be eternal, or everlasting rather, in Scripture, 1. When it is of a long duration, though it will have an end…[or] 2. When a thing hath no end, though it hath a beginning. So angels and [human] souls are everlasting…"[14] Like Augustine and Aquinas, Charnock conceded the point that Scripture itself, when it depicts God as everlasting, does not refer to a time-less state, but simply to indefinitely extended time.

We move on to the subject of immutability. Since God is simple and also immutable, it follows that God's immutability is identical with his being:

> God is unchangeable in his essence, nature, and perfections. Immutability and eternity are linked together; and, indeed, true eternity is true immutability; whence eternity is defined [as] the possession of an immutable life. Yet immutability differs from eternity in our conception; immutability respects the essence or existence of a thing; eternity respects the duration of a being in that state, or rather, immutability is the state itself; eternity is the measure of that state. A thing is said to be changed, when it is otherwise now in regard of nature, state, will, or any quality than it was before; when either something is added to it, or taken from it; when it either loses or acquires. But now it is the essential property of God, not to have any accession to, or diminution of, his essence or attributes, but to remain entirely the same. He wants nothing; he loses nothing; but doth uniformly exist by

14 Charnock, *Attributes*, 1.280.

> himself, without any new nature, new thoughts, new will, new purpose, or new place.[15]

Charnock's main point is that God's character does not change. He doesn't learn new things or deviate from his established purposes. So far, all agree. Yet Charnock also includes in the definition of change, changes of states and qualities. This seems more problematic.

For example, normally we think that God became a creator (i.e., entered into a state of creating and took upon himself the quality of being a creator) upon the creation of this world of ours. The natural assumption is that God was not a creator before creating; rather, he became a creator by creating. This everyday conception assumes time, of course. But God's atemporal, time-less state is strictly unchanging according to Charnock. Charnock must thus affirm that God has always been a creator:

> Nor is there any new relation acquired by God by the creation of the world. There was a new relation acquired by the creature, as, when a man sins, he hath another relation to God than he had before,—he hath relation to God, as a criminal to a Judge; but there is no change in God, but in the malefactor. The being of men makes no more change in God than the sins of men. As a tree is now on our right hand, and by our turning about it is on our left hand, sometimes before us, sometimes behind us, according to our motion near it or about it, and the turning of the body; there is no change in the tree, which remains firm and fixed in the earth, but the change is wholly in the posture of the body, whereby the tree may be said to be before us or behind us, or on the right hand or on the left hand. God gained no new relation of Lord or Creator by the creation; for though he had created

15 Charnock, *Attributes*, 1.317.

> nothing to rule over, yet he had the power to create and rule, though he did not create and rule: as a man may be called a skilful writer, though he does not write, because he is able to do it when he pleases; or a man skilful in physic is called a physician, though he doth not practise that skill, or discover his art in the distribution of medicines, because he may do it when he pleases; it depends upon his own will to show his art when he has a mind to it. So the name Creator and Lord belongs to God from eternity, because he could create and rule, though he did not create and rule.[16]

It seems a strange world the classical theist lives in whereby a man may be a great writer who has never written anything, or a great physician who has never practiced medicine. According to Charnock, creation brought about no change in God, and thus God was always a creator. Likewise, God was always a savior. Charnock's reason for holding this view is evident: in a static situation, God could always be a creator or never be a creator, but he cannot change his status in the middle for then he would not be strictly immutable.

Yet from the human vantage point of time, to imagine that God supposed himself a creator before anything was created and a savior before anyone was saved seems to make God something very far from omniscient. God must certainly know that, with respect to time, he wasn't a creator before he created anything and wasn't a savior before saving anyone. If he doesn't understand that concept as we understand it, then he certainly doesn't know all that can be known. To say that God is omniscient but doesn't know time, as time, is to say he is all-knowing and yet doesn't know something that even the simplest simpleton here on earth is very well aware of.

A God without varying states or qualities would seemingly also be strictly unrelatable. The illustration of God as a static tree in the midst

16 Charnock, *Attributes*, 1.339.

of a field suggests as much. The tree, of course, does not and cannot personally relate with those moving about it. Those moving about the tree form a new relation, but not so the tree itself.

For us, we experience a conversion that brings about a change of relation to God. From our Christian perspective, God was an angry judge prior to our conversion, but then he became a loving father. Of course, an immutable, changeless, time-less being could not experience this sort of dynamic change. From his divine perspective, it is said that never a change occurs. It seems, then, impossible to determine whether this means that God was always my loving father or never my loving father. Perhaps even more dreadful is the thought that God, in his "eternal now," is both presently an angry judge to me and presently a loving father to me. If God sees all as present, then I am presumably both presently redeemed and presently unredeemed from his unique vantage point.

Curiously, Charnock seemed to go in an entirely different direction when speaking of God's sovereignty, allowing that you cannot be a "sovereign" until there's actually something to be sovereign over:

> [His dominion] is an eternal dominion. In regard of the exercise of it, it was not from eternity, because there was not from eternity any creature under the government of it; but in regard of the foundation of it, his essence, his excellency, it is eternal; as God was from eternity almighty, but there was no exercise or manifestation of it till he began to create.[17]

Ignoring the inconsistency, if God is *absolutely* immutable, that is, unchanging in every conceivable sense of the word "change," then it would seem to follow that he cannot form new relationships or new actions. Charnock concedes the point that the creation was not a new action on God's part:

---

17 Charnock, *Attributes*, 2.386.

> There was no change in God when he began to create the world in time. The creation was a real change, but the change was not subjectively in God, but in the creature; the creature began to be what it was not before.... There was no change in God by the act of creation, because there was no new will in him. There was no new act of his will which was not before. The creation began in time, but the will of creating was from eternity. The work was new, but the *decree* whence that new work sprung was as ancient as the Ancient of Days. When the time of creating came...whatsoever God willed to be now done, he willed from eternity to be done; but he willed also that it should not be done till such an instant of time, and that it should not exist before such a time.[18]

Charnock (following the great Reformer, John Calvin [1509-1564]) imagined that God time-lessly issued a divine "decree" from his time-less eternity. This decree apparently included the precise details about the time at which creation would begin, the manner in which creation would unfold, and so forth. It's not so much that God created the world directly, but indirectly by his divine and eternal decree.

The divine decree was conceived of as an impersonal and unstoppable directive from God. God shouts his kingly orders from his time-less eternity, resulting in a decree that, unlike himself, is operative in time. By this reasoning, though God does not operate directly in time, his decree can do his temporal work in his stead.

It should be noted that Charnock's "decree" serves the exact same function that angels served in the systems of Augustine, Dionysius, and Aquinas. The divine decree does the dirty work of operating in time, where God himself is imagined as incapable of doing so. The Reformers had little patience for unfounded, Scholastic conjectures about angelic abilities, yet still felt the need to posit some intermediary between the

18 Charnock, *Attributes*, 1.337.

time-less God and the temporal world. The "decree" filled precisely the same void. Of course, this helps us to avoid the sticky question as to how angels are able to traverse the boundary between time-lessness and time, but at what cost? We are now governed not by God himself, but by an impersonal force, like something out of *Star Wars*.

Other problems seem to compound quickly. How could a simple God issue a very complicated, non-simple decree? Would not the decree of the simple God itself be simple and, therefore, identical with God? Would not God shouting his decree into time itself take time to carry out? More significantly, God hardly seems to be all-powerful if he cannot operate directly inside of time. You and I can operate directly inside of time, of course. I do things in time all the time. If God cannot do so, then obviously I can do something which God can't do, yet that hardly seems a proper depiction of omnipotence.

Another important question is, does this impersonal decree actually solve the original problem? If we are to imagine that the simple and time-less God created a complex, temporal decree, could we not just skip the decree altogether and say that God himself directly created and governs the complex, temporal world? I like to think that God *himself* listens to my temporal prayers without the mediation of an impersonal decree. It's not at all clear how positing an impersonal force between the immutable God and his mutable creation actually improves the situation. Charnock is still trying to multiply intermediaries in order to ease the tension inherent in the Neoplatonic scheme of classical theism. He's still trying to find a way around the Platonic Divorce, but it's all smoke and mirrors.

We move on to God's simplicity. As simple, God is identical to his own knowledge:

> God knows by his own essence. ...He hath not an understanding distinct from his essence as we have, but being the most simple Being, his understanding is his essence; and as from the infiniteness of his essence we conclude the

> infiniteness of his understanding, so from the unchangeableness of his essence, we may justly conclude the unchangeableness of his knowledge. Since, therefore, God is without all composition, and his understanding is not distinct from his essence, what he knows, he knows by his essence, and there can then be no more mutability in his knowledge than there can be in his essence... If his understanding and his essence were not one and the same, he were not simple, but compounded: if compounded, he would consist of parts; if he consisted of parts, he would not be an independent Being, and so would not be God.[19]

God is identical to his own knowledge, and God's knowledge is immutable like God himself. Charnock is certainly no pantheist, yet still the question seems to me unanswered, if God is identical to his knowledge and his knowledge encompasses a knowledge of creation, is not God identical to his creation? Plotinus seems to me to have really been the most consistent of the classical theists.

God's power and wisdom are, likewise, one and the same thing, identical with God.[20] "He is so wise, that he is wisdom itself."[21] Charnock goes on to define wisdom as acting with discretion and prudence.[22] This is troublesome. If God is identical to wisdom, and wisdom is acting with discretion and prudence, then it seems to follow—as a plain matter of definition—that God is identical to acting with discretion and prudence. God, on that account, would seemingly be an action rather than a personal being, which is, of course, absurd.

The problem here is evident. For us, wisdom is, roughly, taking the right course of action under the circumstances that present themselves.

---

19 Charnock, *Attributes*, 1.323.

20 Charnock, *Attributes*, 1.383.

21 Charnock, *Attributes*, 1.506.

22 See Charnock, *Attributes*, 1.507.

Wisdom in normal, everyday usage is not a being, but a sort of decision-making strategy. To us, wisdom is purely abstract and conceptual. Yet when we say that God is identical to wisdom, as such, we cannot mean that God is identical to a conceptual decision-making strategy. "Wisdom," as we know it, is not a concrete being, but something much more like a procedure or thought process. Yet the "wisdom" that is identical to God is obviously a personal being, but we humans have no experience of the sort of wisdom that is identical to a personal being. That sort of wisdom is unknown to us. The problem, then, is that as soon as we say something like "God is identical to wisdom, as such" we have to simultaneously concede the point that we don't know what we mean by the expression, and that it is, in fact, meaningless to us. It seems a case of pure mysticism, for the expression communicates no definite information. God is wise, to be sure, but to say that God is identical to wisdom itself is, in my estimation, a profound confusion. A very strong form of realism about "wisdom" has clearly run amuck. We have tried to turn a concept into a person, to reify an abstract descriptive term into a concrete being. Basically, we have tried to turn God into one of Plato's Forms.

Admittedly, God is called wisdom in several instances in Scripture. Christ is called "the power of God and the wisdom of God," for example, in 1 Corinthians 1:24. For my part, I don't for a moment think Paul meant that Christ is identical to wisdom and power, as such, in the sense the classical theist requires. Rather, Paul meant that accepting Christ is the wise course for man which also empowers man unto spiritual life. In other words, Paul means that Christ is *our* wisdom and power, not wisdom and power, as such. He meant that by following Christ, we wisely tap into God's unlimited power. This reading gives the text a practical relevance where the realist interpretation of classical theism leads simply to endless head-scratching regarding how a person could literally be identical to a sound course of action.

Simplicity inevitably blurs the line between God's being and actions. Charnock says, in one place, that God's power "is not distinct from his essence" and that "it is his essence as operative."[23] Yet, to be consistent with simplicity, it would have to be conceded that God's simple "essence as operative" is identical to his essence, period, that is, identical to his essence without any further qualifications. Thus God, identical to his essence, would also be identical to God's essence, imagined as operative. Thus God would be identical to his own actions and operations. Thus, God and the creation would be identical.

A simple God could presumably not make a sharp distinction between being and acting. Seemingly, a simple God could not make any distinctions at all. God cannot merely act wisely, but must be wisdom itself. God cannot merely possess knowledge, but must be knowledge itself. It would also seem to follow that God must be identical to his own patience, his own long-suffering, and so forth. God would also be identical to his own creative act. In one place, Charnock seems to allow it:

> God, indeed, by one simple act, knows himself and the creatures; but when that act whereby he knows himself, is conceived by us to pass to the knowledge of the creatures, we must not understand it to be a new act, distinct from the other; but the same act upon different terms or objects; such an order is in our understandings and conceptions, not in God's.[24]

The simple act by which God knows himself is the same simple act by which God knows his creatures. Charnock is certainly no pantheist, but this seems to me pantheistic in principle. Though we normally think of God's knowledge of his creation as something quite distinct

23 Charnock, *Attributes*, 2.17.

24 Charnock, *Attributes*, 1.454.

from himself, a simple God cannot be distinct from any aspect of his own knowledge. God's knowledge of creatures would be identical to his knowledge of himself. Likewise, a simple God would seemingly be incapable of distinguishing other beings from his own being.

We normally think of God as having a knowledge of us much like we have a knowledge of him. In our case, it's clear that God occupies a part of our individual brains. This or that part of my brain stores information about God. Normally, we also think that God thinks about us likewise, namely, that he has a store of information about each of us, and that each of us forms some part of his knowledge. Yet nothing can be partial for a God without parts. We cannot take up a part of his consciousness, for it has no parts. Whatever God knows must be identical to God or else God is not simple. God must know me in such a way that his knowledge of me is identical to his knowledge of himself, but that results in pantheism.[25]

God's knowledge of me would seemingly also be an immutable knowledge. He could presumably not be aware that I am writing this book in the present, for the writing of this book is a long series of mutations. The whole process is mutable, from beginning to end. I type out a lousy sentence and then read and re-read, refining each time, hoping for the (unlikely) outcome that the end result is clear and persuasive. What would it possibly mean to have an immutable knowledge of a mutable process? The two are simply incompatible with one another. The two are dualistic and antithetical to one another, by definition.

As simple, God is identical to his own existence, according to Charnock.[26] Yet, as Dionysius seemed to imply, if humans exist and if existence itself is identical to God, then my existence would seemingly be identical to the existence of God.

---

25 To be crystal clear, I have no sympathies with pantheism. I am merely arguing that classical theism would logically result in a pantheism like that of Plotinus if it was taken to its logical and consistent end.

26 Charnock, *Attributes*, 1.333.

The simple God is also identical to his own will.[27] Numerous contemporary commentators have noted that classical theism seems, in this regard, to present God with a free will problem. If God exists necessarily, and his will is identical to his existence, then his individual choices would be every bit as *necessary* as his existence itself is. Since God is identical to his own choices, he cannot *choose* otherwise any more than he can *be* otherwise, for his being and will are really one and the same thing. His choices would be as immutable and unchangeable as his being. His choices would always be of necessity. He could never choose otherwise than he does choose. This problem is further compounded by the fact that the future is already firmly fixed in place in God's immutable "eternal now." Such a situation seems to preclude the possibility of free choices in a dynamic scheme.

In some instances, Charnock seems to forget the law of divine simplicity. He says, for example,

> Every law, though it consists in an act of the will, yet doth presuppose an act of the understanding. The act of the Divine understanding in framing the law, must be supposed to precede the act of his will in commanding the observance of that law.[28]

Charnock's suggestion that God's understanding of the law logically precedes his commandment for us to obey it implies a sharp distinction between God's understanding and will. Yet Charnock has already insisted that God's understanding and will are one and the same as far as God is concerned. If God's simple understanding is identical to his simple will, then it is plainly nonsensical to say that one precedes the other, at least as far as God himself is concerned.

27 Charnock, *Attributes*, 1.325.

28 Charnock, *Attributes*, 1.586.

When speaking of the power of God, Charnock is insistent that the creation demonstrates a partial use of God's power.[29] If God "could do no more than what he hath done, his power would be finite."[30] Charnock here seems to imagine that when God created the world, he used part of his power to do so. God need not use all of his power to create the world; rather, he used some portion of his power.

Yet this is inconsistent with simplicity. A simple God has no parts, and could not use *part* of his power. God's power would be simple and, therefore, strictly indivisible. God's power would be nothing more and nothing less than God himself. God's power would be atomic in the original, Greek sense of indivisible, uncuttable, or unsplittable. God could not use his power partially, for God has no parts and his power is identical to himself. So it would seem to be impossible for the simple God to use only part of his power to create the world.

Elsewhere, Charnock seems to hesitate a bit and says that God's power is "not really distinct"[31] from his wisdom, though they seem to us distinct. In such a situation, it seems that we are *not really* talking about God at all when we distinguish between God's wisdom and power. It is a bit curious, after all, to write a 2,000-page book about God's "attributes" when God, in fact, does not have attributes.

Charnock said that God is identical to his goodness. He is "not only good, but goodness itself, the supreme inconceivable goodness."[32] God is goodness, as such, "good *per se.*"[33]

> Goodness is not a quality in him, but a nature; not a habit added to his essence, but his essence itself; he is not first God, and then afterwards good; but he is good as he is God; his essence, being one and the same, is formally and equally

29 See Charnock, *Attributes*, 2.12.

30 Charnock, *Attributes*, 2.21.

31 Charnock, *Attributes*, 2.14.

32 Charnock, *Attributes*, 2.211.

33 Charnock, *Attributes*, 2.221.

> God and good. Αυιάγαθον, "good of himself," was one of the names the Platonists gave him. He is essentially good in his own nature, and not by any outward action which follows his essence. He is an independent Being, and hath nothing of goodness or happiness from anything without him, or anything he doth act about. If he were not good by his essence, he could not be eternally good, he could not be the first good; he would have something before him, from whence he derived that goodness wherewith he is possessed; nor could he be perfectly good, for he could not be equally good to that from whom he derived his goodness; no star, no splendid body, that derives light from the sun, doth equal that sun by which it is enlightened. ...He is essentially good by his own essence; therefore, good of himself; therefore, eternally good; and therefore, abundantly good.[34]

This passage provides a relatively clear argument as to why Charnock believes that God must be simple. We saw roughly the same argument made by Aquinas. If God were not identical to goodness, then he must derive his goodness from some other source. God "hath goodness by participation from no other, but originally from himself."[35] As was the case with Aquinas, the weakness of the argument rests in the fact that it requires a very strong form of realism about goodness. It requires that we think of "goodness" as a concrete entity, much like a Platonic Form. Charnock even expressly notes that the Platonists taught precisely the same doctrine.

Charnock is clearly a strong realist as to goodness. Goodness is, by this account, a personal being. Presumably, we may pray to Goodness and worship Goodness. Presumably, "The Good" is God, after all. Yet Charnock goes on to define God's goodness primarily in terms of

34 Charnock, *Attributes*, 2.221.

35 Charnock, *Attributes*, 2.222.

God's benevolence. When we say that God is good, in most cases, we mean that he is merciful and kind to us. We mean that God is benevolent, that he benefits us, as it were. Charnock defined goodness in one place as "whatsoever is comely, excellent, desirable."[36] Yet if goodness is comeliness and desirability, and God is identical to goodness, obviously it follows that God is identical to excellence, comeliness, and desirability.

The normal dictionary definition of these words would suggest to us that they do not depict concrete objects. Rather, these words depict abstract ideas. Take "excellence," for example. To be excellent is, of course, to excel at something, where excelling at something is to be proficient at it. A person can excel at archery, or making money from the stock market, or gardening, or what have you. A person can also have an excellent character or an excellent beauty, by which we mean that they have that quality to a greater extent than others of the same kind. Given the normal dictionary definition of excellence, then, it's obvious that excellence is merely an abstract evaluation of proficiency. As such, humans can *demonstrate* excellence, but it would entail tremendous confusion to say that such and such person *is excellence itself*. Such an expression would be meaningless.

Similarly, words like "good" and "bad" are very generic words we use to express our general like or dislike, favor or disfavor of this or that. Most often, we use the word "good" as an adjective expressing approval, and the word "bad" as an adjective expressing disapproval. Good ice cream is preferable to bad ice cream; a good spouse is preferable to a bad spouse, and so on. The terms "good" and "bad" do not represent any particular concrete object, of course. We don't expect to see someone's picture when we look up the definition of the word "good" or "bad." We don't expect any particular person or object to be described in the definition. We all understand, I think, that the words

36 Charnock, *Attributes*, 2.214.

"good" and "bad" are very generic words that can be used flexibly in various contexts. It's a generic, descriptive term that doesn't really tell us about what an object is, but more about whether we approve of it or not.

So Charnock's argument that God must be goodness itself if God is to maintain his independence completely fails if we merely say that "goodness" is only a conceptual, evaluative word. Charnock, following Plato and other strong realists, is trying his best to turn "goodness" into a proper noun rather than merely an abstract, evaluative, comparative word, but this is a confusion.

If God is strictly and literally goodness, then it would seem to follow that we must also require that God is strictly and literally sovereignty itself, and strictly and literally long-suffering itself, and strictly and literally hatred of sin itself, and so on. Classical theists tend to ignore inconvenient conclusions such as these, however necessary they may be as far as logical consistency is concerned.

Charnock said that "all things are good by a participation" in God's goodness,[37] and that we should strive to imitate God's goodness.[38] Yet that seems quite clearly an impossibility within the scheme of classical theism, for we certainly cannot become identical to goodness itself. In the scheme of classical theism, our goodness would be of a qualitatively different type than God's goodness, in which case, we could hardly imitate his goodness.

We move on to impassibility. Charnock denied that the immutable and simple God ever experiences transient emotions:

> God is a pure Spirit, and is not capable of those passions which are signs of weakness and impotence, or subject to those regrets we are subject to. …God doth not act but upon clear and infallible reason; and a change upon passion

37 Charnock, *Attributes*, 2.346.

38 Charnock, *Attributes*, 2.353.

> is accounted by all so great a weakness in man, that none can entertain so unworthy a conceit of God. Where he is said to repent (Gen. 6:6), he is also said to grieve; now no proper grief can be imagined to be in God. As repentance is inconsistent with infallible foresight, so is grief no less inconsistent with undefiled blessedness. God is "blessed forever" (Rom. 9:8), and therefore nothing can befall him that can stain that blessedness. …But God accommodates himself in the Scripture to our weak capacity. God hath no more of a proper repentance, than he hath of a real body; though he, in accommodation to our weakness, ascribes to himself the members of our bodies to set out to our understanding the greatness of his perfections, we must not conclude him a body like us; so, because he is said to have anger and repentance, we must not conclude him to have passions like us. When we cannot fully comprehend him as he is, he clothes himself with our nature in his expressions that we may apprehend him as we are able, and by an inspection into ourselves, learn something of the nature of God; yet those human ways of speaking ought to be understood in a manner agreeable to the infinite excellency and majesty of God, and are only designed to mark out something in God which hath a *resemblance* with something in us; as we cannot speak to God as gods, but as men, so we cannot understand him speaking to us as a God, unless he condescend to speak to us like a man.[39]

So for roughly the same reason that we shouldn't take Scripture's presentation of God having a body with strict literality, so too we shouldn't take God's emotions with strict literality. According to Charnock, God, in himself, does not actually experience the emotional

39 Charnock, *Attributes*, 1.340-341.

highs and lows ascribed to him in Scripture. A temporary state of anger, for example, is inconsistent with God's time-less and immutable blessedness. Therefore, the biblical depiction of God as angry, exuberant, joyful, jealous, etc., at this or that time, upon this or that occasion, is, in every instance, an accommodation to the weakness of man. God speaks to us as if he were a man, though he is not a man.

That the Bible sometimes makes accommodations to man must be granted. No theologian would take such expressions of the flaring nostrils or strong arm of the Lord with strict literality. God presents himself, in those instances, as if he were a man. This much must be granted. The biblical context itself often indicates, in such cases, that metaphors are being deployed. In the case of the "strong arm" of the Lord, for instance, the parallel between God and man is obvious. As a man uses his physical strength to affect change—to plow a field or build a house—so too God can and does exert power to shape the course of events. He created the world by his power and sustains the world by his power. The resemblance between God and man, in such a case, is natural and obvious.

Charnock says that Scripture's portrayal of God as emotional is, likewise, to point us to a "resemblance" between God and man. The weakness of this view, it seems to me, lies in the question, where exactly is the resemblance? Man gets angry. That much we know. But if God does not experience anger, where is the resemblance? As far as I can see, there is no resemblance. Man gets angry, but God is incapable of anger, for this contradicts his perpetual blessedness, according to Charnock. That hardly seems a resemblance.

Charnock might respond that the resemblance rests in the fact that God would get angry if God were a man. A man's righteous anger is justified before God because God would do the same if God were a man subject to emotions like anger. This hardly answers the objection, however. Let me rephrase the question: what do I learn about God *himself* from all of those biblical passages that depict him as angry, rejoicing, and so on? Charnock seems to be of the opinion, as far as I can tell, that we don't learn anything about what God is like from those passages. We really only learn what man is like. As with Aquinas' "analogical" knowledge, the alleged analogy turns out to be no analogy at all.

It seems to me a very curious canon of biblical interpretation that says when we read that God is angry in Scripture, we should take this to mean that God is incapable of anger. To be frank, this seems less an "interpretation" and more a manifest rejection of what Scripture plainly says.

Of course, impassibility is consistent with Charnock's classical theism. An immutable God cannot get angry, for the transition would represent a change of state, the taking upon himself a new quality. Nor could a time-less God get angry, for a transitory anger supposes a transitory passage through time. Nor could a simple God get angry, for a simple God cannot experience a manifold variety of emotional states. Classical theism must be embraced as a whole or rejected as a whole. Yet must not every Bible teacher speak as if God has strong emotions? Charnock the pastor certainly seems to do so:

> How meltingly doth [God] bewail man's wilful refusal of his goodness! ...He seems to utter those words in a sigh, "O that my people had hearkened unto me, and Israel had walked in my way" (Psalm 81:13)! It is true, God hath not human passions, but his affections cannot be expressed otherwise in a way intelligible to us; the excellency of his nature is above the passions of men; but such expressions of himself manifest to us the sincerity of his goodness: and that, were he capable of our passions, he would express himself in such a manner as we do: and we find incarnate Goodness bewailing with tears and sighs the ruin of Jerusalem (Luke 19:42). By the same reason that when

> a sinner returns there is joy in heaven, upon his obstinacy there is sorrow in earth.[40]

Charnock said that God does not have "human passions." This seems a sleight of hand. Does he then, perhaps, have divine passions? Charnock would undoubtedly answer in the negative. God would have passions if he were human, but he is not human, and thus does not actually have passions. God describes himself as passionate though he is actually passion-less to "manifest to us the sincerity of his goodness." It hardly seems like sincerity, however, to consistently present yourself as something that you are not. Charnock insisted that there is joy in heaven when a sinner repents, but, of course, we must conclude that it cannot be God rejoicing, for joy is quite obviously a passion, and the expression of joy is obviously a temporal phenomenon.

Charnock closes the work with a chapter on God's patience. He insists that God is not emotional, yet also uses countless terms indicative of strong emotion:

> Slowness to anger, or admirable patience, is the property of the Divine nature. As patience signifies suffering, so it is not in God. The Divine nature is impassible, incapable of any impair, it cannot be touched by the violences of men, nor the essential glory of it be diminished by the injuries of men; but as it signifies a willingness to defer, and an unwillingness to pour forth his wrath upon sinful creatures, he moderates his provoked justice, and forbears to revenge the injuries he daily meets with in the world. He suffers no grief by men's wronging him, but he restrains his arm from punishing them according to their merits; and thus there is patience in every cross a man meets with in the world, because, though it be a punishment, it is less than is merited by the

40 Charnock, *Attributes*, 2.286.

> unrighteous rebel, and less than may be inflicted by a righteous and powerful God.[41]

Charnock said that God has no emotions, yet also seemed to present him as highly emotional. Notice how many emotionally charged words are used in this paragraph. God cannot be touched by man, but must nevertheless restrain his "wrath." One wonders, why is he wrathful if he cannot be touched? Likewise, his justice is "provoked." But why is he provoked unto justice if not personally offended in some way? Charnock said that God "forbears to revenge the injuries he daily meets with in the world" though he cannot be emotionally injured. It seems to me altogether unclear why God must restrain himself if not offended in the first place. Why must there be vengeance if no offense? Why retribution upon man if all is endless, changeless bliss and blessedness for God? It seems morally indefensible for God to make a pretense of offense if there is, in reality, no offense as far as God's changeless and impassible emotional state is concerned.

In some instances, Charnock seems to completely forget that God is without passions:

> [God] is "slow to anger;" the prophet doth not say, he is incapable of anger, or cannot discern what is a real object of anger; it implies, that he doth consider every provocation, but he is not hasty to discharge his arrows upon the offenders; he sees all, while he bears with them; his omniscience excludes any ignorance; he cannot but see every wrong; every aggravation in that wrong, every step and motion from the beginning to the completing it; for he knows all our thoughts; he sees the sin and the sinner at the same time; the sin with an eye of abhorrency, and the sinner with an eye of pity. His eye is upon their iniquities, and his hatred edged

41 Charnock, *Attributes*, 2.477.

> against them; while he stands with arms open, waiting a penitent return.[42]

Charnock here requires that God is capable of anger, offense, aggravation, abhorrence, pity, etc. Once again, it is not always easy to reconcile the academic and pastoral Charnock.

His overall position is clear, however: Charnock was a classical theist. On account of God's time-lessness, simplicity, and immutability, Charnock allowed that God is, in the last analysis, unknowable to us:

> Whatsoever hath limits and is changeable, is conceivable and searchable; but *God is not only not known, but impossible in his own nature to be known* and searched out, and, therefore, impossible to have any diminution in his nature. All that which is changed arrives to something which it was not before, or ceaseth in part to be what it was before.[43]

Even if we suppose the classical theist to be correct in his estimation of God, we simultaneously disallow that he has any actual knowledge of God. In other words, even if he is correct about God, he knows nothing about God by his own admission. Seemingly, he is wrong about God even if he is right about God.

Though not always with perfect consistency, Charnock was most definitely committed to upholding the essential elements of classical theism. He clearly believed that God is simple, time-less, impassible, and absolutely immutable. However, on some occasions, his thought seems to be pressed in quite a different direction. When speaking of man being made in the image of God, Charnock draws many parallels between God and man. "If God made man according to his image, we must raise our thoughts of God according to the noblest part of that

---

42 Charnock, *Attributes*, 2.480.

43 Charnock, *Attributes*, 1.334.

image, and imagine the exemplar…not to come short, but to exceed the thing copied by it."[44] As made in God's image, man is seemingly modeled after God, and man can infer truths about God from his own nature. According to Charnock, the image of God in man is seen principally in man's sovereignty over creation and the "spiritual faculties of the soul" such as man's intelligence and ability to emulate God in moral rectitude.[45]

In the section on God's holiness, Charnock similarly argued that the Christian is renewed in God's image and imitates God's holiness. Significant emphasis is placed upon our similarity to God, as bearing God's very image:

> As election is the effect of God's sovereignty, our pardon the fruit of his mercy, our knowledge a stream from his wisdom, our strength an impression of his power; so our purity is a beam from his holiness.[46]

There seems an obvious tension here. The *imago dei* doctrine naturally invites a comparison of God's attributes and man's attributes. Man is made to be like God and is, therefore, like God. Yet classical theism requires an apophatic and definitive contrast, a comprehensive epistemological divorce.

Charnock seemed to fluctuate between two different conceptions of theology. He often exploited the ambiguity of various theological terms. The ambiguity of the word "eternity" I have already mentioned. Similarly, a term such as "incomprehensible" in some places only seems to mean that God cannot be known *comprehensively*, but, on other occasions, seems to suggest that God cannot be understood at all, on even the most rudimentary level. A term such as "immutable" can mean either that God doesn't change in personal character or, alternatively,

44 Charnock, *Attributes*, 1.183.

45 Charnock, *Attributes*, 1.191-192.

46 Charnock, *Attributes*, 2.139.

that God is never involved in any sort of change, including even new actions or new relationships. Charnock often seemed to flip-flop in his usage of such terms, thus allowing him to speak at times like a classical theist and, at times, like what I have called a relational theist.

Charnock was undoubtedly a classical theist, but he was also inconsistently so. The academic Charnock and the pastoral Charnock don't always seem to agree. My suggestion is that while the voices of the past were pushing Charnock in one direction, the Reformational emphasis upon *Sola Scriptura* was pushing him in quite another.

10

KARL BARTH

KARL Barth (1886–1968), it now seems clear, was the most influential theologian of the past century. He was also undoubtedly the most controversial. On account of many novel tendencies in Barth's thought, many of his peers labeled him Neo-orthodox. Barth squarely rejected the title; he considered himself Protestant, Evangelical, and Reformed. Barth was quite vocal that, in his own view, he was seeking to purge the Reformational theology of Luther and Calvin of errors that had crept in subsequently, particularly in the seventeenth century.

Barth's orthodoxy on numerous points is still greatly debated. Since his orthodoxy is questionable, his place here may likewise seem questionable. I will try, however, to convince the reader that Barth was a very consistent classical theist. We may well view Barth's thought as a reaction to a thinker like Charnock whose classical theism seemed to be compromised and diluted at various points.

It is fortuitous for our present purpose that Barth returns to the subject of the human knowledge of God again and again throughout his writings. It is clearly a centerpiece of his thought. Barth approached the question with a truly astonishing degree of logical rigor. On the epistemological separation between God and man in the scheme of classical theism, Barth represents the state of the art.

Fundamental to Barth's system is the recurrent and adamant affirmation that God, as God, cannot be known by man in any measure. While man learns about God primarily through the Incarnation of Christ, even in Christ we cannot see God's *proper* divinity, for God's proper divinity is simple and time-less. Since we cannot even begin to understand God's simple and time-less divinity, according to Barth, "God is known only by God; God can be known only by God."[1] This is, of course, a familiar theme.

According to Barth, God is entirely unique, wholly unlike mankind. God is "the altogether Other."[2] God is "other" not just in the sense that he is distinct from his creation, but also in the sense that he is nothing like his creation. At every point, God is distinct from creation and stands in stark contrast to creation:

> That Other from which we have come and which is contrasted with all concrete, known, temporal, human existence can be in no manner wholly distinct unless it be in every manner wholly distinct.[3]

Barth denies that God and man share any common "nexus" of being. It is vain to imagine a "continuity of existence between us and God."[4] As wholly distinct and "other," the simple and time-less God stands in "ineffaceable antithesis to all humanity."[5] Seemingly, we have come full circle as the Greek dualism of antithetical opposites is applied to God and man in its full force. Where God is time-less and man temporal, where God is simple and man manifold, God is

1 Barth, *Dogmatics*, V2.1,5.27.1 (183).
2 Barth, *Romans,* 42.
3 Barth, *Romans,* 115.
4 Barth, *Romans*, 296.
5 Barth, *Dogmatics*, V1.1/1.3.1 (61).

man's polar opposite, by definition. God is man's very antithesis, and vice versa.

Since God and man have nothing in common and stand in epistemological antithesis to one another, human language and logic are inapplicable to God. "Our human views and concepts...have not in themselves the smallest capacity to apprehend God. ...He remains completely unknowable to us..."[6] God is "beyond all experience and thought."[7]

We should not imagine that man is, in any sense, a proper "receptacle" for the knowledge of God. "Human experience and human perception end where God begins."[8] On account of the epistemological uniqueness of God, "There is no direct knowledge of God... It is impossible to lay hold of Him."[9] As occupying a contrary mode of being, man lacks the proper equipment to know anything of God. "We have no organ or capacity for God."[10] Man has no notion of God, as God. Barth asks rhetorically:

> But is God really an object of human cognition? Is an object of human cognition God? No postulate, however necessary, can compel this to be true. ...For without the grace of His revelation, God is definitely not an object of human cognition, and definitely no object of human cognition is God.[11]

Language fails us, logic is altogether inadequate. God "is hidden from us," "cannot be anticipated or repeated in any human word," and

---

6 Barth, *Dogmatics*, V2.1, 6.29.1 (342).

7 Barth, *Dogmatics*, V1.1, 1.5.4 (181).

8 Barth, *Romans*, 120.

9 Barth, *Romans*, 423.

10 Barth, *Dogmatics*, V1.1, 1.5.4 (168).

11 Barth, *Dogmatics*, V2.1, 5.27.2 (206). Barth seems to conflate human cognition of an object with the being of that object, as if to say that to possess a knowledge of God would imply that God himself is identical with our individual conception of God. This seems to be a straw man.

"cannot be adequately rendered in any human word."[12] God "cannot be the object of one of those perceptions to which our concepts, our thought-forms and finally our words and sentences are related."[13]

Barth agrees with Clement of Alexandria that God is invisible to man not just physically, but also spiritually and epistemologically. God is invisible to us in every sense of the word:

> Of ourselves we do not resemble God. We are not master of God. We are not one with God. We are not capable of conceiving Him. But this means, with a backward reference so to speak, in respect of the views to which our concepts must be related, that no man has ever seen God. …God is invisible. He is invisible to the physical eye of man; He is also invisible to the so-called spiritual. He is not identical with any of the objects which can become the content of the images of our external or inner perception.[14]

Barth here suggests that the apostolic teaching that "no one has seen God at any time" (John 1:18) means that no one has ever known anything of God, as God. Properly speaking, man has neither experience of God nor knowledge of God; God is "incomprehensible and unexperienced."[15] The human attempt to search out God-in-himself is altogether vain:

> This search is not one that should be pursued further and further into every new and hitherto unknown or even undreamed of area of human reality, no matter whether it is a matter of new positions or merely of the possible limits of

---

12 Barth, *Dogmatics*, V1.1, 1.5.2 (132).

13 Barth, *Dogmatics*, V2.1, 5.27.1 (186).

14 Barth, *Dogmatics*, V2.1, 5.27.1 (190).

15 Barth, *Romans*, 316.

> this or that or even all possible positions. The insight that is needed here is that this search is pointless.[16]

Though most theologians hope to learn something about God, as God, it is part of the task of theology, according to Barth, to point out that such a task is sinful and misdirected, an "illegitimate yearning."[17] Since God and man do not occupy the same "plane," theology must begin by "de-assuring" us of a knowledge of God. This is "a theological warning against theology."[18] Theology must begin with this strong renunciation: "It is in faith itself that we are forced to dispossess ourselves of any capacity for viewing and conceiving God."[19] Christian faith, according to Barth, should begin upon the premise that God, as such, cannot be known by us. For Barth, God is revealed to us in Christ, to be sure, but, as we will see, even in Christ we do not obtain a *proper* knowledge of God.

Barth is thus quite comfortable speaking of an epistemological divide between God and man. Barth contrasts nature and grace, where "nature," in Barth's usage, refers to man's side of the divide (i.e., man's mode of being) and grace refers to "God's side."[20] Thus it is clear that Barth accepts the traditional divide between God and man which I have characterized as Platonic and Neoplatonic in character.

Barth imagines two discrete worlds in contrast with one another: "We who stand in this concrete world know nothing, and are incapable of knowing anything, of that other world."[21] There is an unbridgeable separation between God and man. "The Being and Action of God are and remain wholly different from the being and action of men.

16 Barth, *Dogmatics*, V1.1, 1.5.4 (184).

17 Barth, *Dogmatics*, V1.1, 1.5.4 (164).

18 Barth, *Dogmatics*, V1.1, 1.5.4 (165).

19 Barth, *Dogmatics*, V2.1, 5.27.1 (184-185). Also, V1.1, 1.5.4 (185).

20 See Barth, *Dogmatics*, V1.2, 2.13.2 (37).

21 Barth, *Romans*, 30.

The line which separates here from there cannot be crossed…"[22] The divorce is comprehensive.

With less optimism and more consistency than Aquinas, Barth says that even after death we will still not know or see anything of God. "God as God, in Himself, will still be hidden from us even then."[23] All creatures, including angels, share this necessary limitation, inherent to all created reality. The chasm between God and man shall never be overcome, and it is foolish to try.

Barth agrees with Plato that God is pure *being*. In the Incarnation, we see "self-moved being in the stream of becoming."[24] Barth agrees with Aristotle that God is pure actuality.[25]

Barth affirms God's "absolute simplicity."[26] This is, of course, consistent with his affirmation that God cannot be known, and gives strong impetus in that direction. In his exposition of the doctrine of God, Barth—like Aquinas—places simplicity first among God's attributes both chronologically and logically. Each of God's attributes, in Barth's treatment, begins with a reminder that it is, in reality, identical to each of God's other attributes.

As in Aquinas, the simplicity doctrine largely determines the course of the entire system. A simple God cannot be known by the manifold, non-simple human mind. Our brains are full of distinctions; God knows no distinctions. Therefore, God and man stand in epistemic antithesis to one another. Barth acknowledges that his view of simplicity is formally the same as that of Aquinas and the Scholastics generally.[27]

---

22 Barth, *Romans*, 111.

23 See Barth, *Dogmatics*, V2.1, 5.27.2 (209).

24 Barth, *Dogmatics*, V1.1, 1.4.3 (116).

25 Barth, *Dogmatics*, V2.1, 6.28.1 (264).

26 Barth, *Dogmatics*, V1.1, 2.12.2 (483).

27 Barth, *Dogmatics*, V2.1, 6.29.1 (350).

Subject and predicate are all one in God.[28] Barth continually reminds us that God does not have a plurality of attributes, properly speaking.[29] "Every individual perfection in God is nothing but God Himself and therefore nothing but every other divine perfection."[30] Accordingly, God is identical with his eternity.[31]

On account of his simplicity, God cannot be known partially. Here again, Barth is more consistent than Aquinas. A being that has no parts cannot be known partially. To know God at all would necessitate that we know him exhaustively. "We either know God Himself and therefore entirely, or we do not know Him at all."[32] Barth agrees with Plotinus that to *know* God would be to *be* God. Barth easily evades Plotinus' pantheism by simply denying that we know anything of God. We know nothing of God-in-himself now, nor will we ever know anything of God-in-himself. Barth argues that since the simple God does not actually have a plurality of divine attributes, the way we order and organize the attributes of God in our human theological writings is necessarily arbitrary and pragmatic.[33]

Barth notes—quite insightfully—that the doctrine of simplicity is still a *human* notion. Given that it is a human idea, inevitably rooted in the manifold complexity of human thought, it is not, in any way, identical to the simplicity of God-in-himself. Our notion of simplicity does not and cannot correspond to God's actual simplicity.[34]

Barth has here surely made a correct inference. When theologians assert the "divine simplicity" they are still necessarily doing so within the human mode. Given the assumption of an epistemological

28 Barth, *Dogmatics*, V2.1, 6.28.3 (300).

29 See Barth, *Dogmatics*, V2.1, 6.30.2 (375).

30 Barth, *Dogmatics*, V2.1, 6.29.1 (333).

31 Barth, *Dogmatics*, V2.1, 6.31.3 (639).

32 Barth, *Dogmatics*, V2.1, 5.25.2 (52).

33 See Barth, *Dogmatics*, V2.1, 6.30.1 (352).

34 Barth, *Dogmatics*, V2.1, 6.31.1 (450).

divide between God and man, what a human asserts cannot properly be *divine* simplicity. The human assertion of divine simplicity is still merely a human assertion that cannot actually apply to God himself.

This is quite a brilliant (albeit uncomfortable) insight and demonstrates the depths of Barth's logical rigor. To the extent that the human doctrine of simplicity is alleged to report something about God, as God, we have merely deluded ourselves. To the extent that divine simplicity is intelligible to mankind, it is clearly not *divine* simplicity! To the extent theologians have imagined that they were talking about God himself when they spoke of divine simplicity, they were merely confused. Augustine and Aquinas were undoubtedly held captive under the sway of this strong delusion.

Barth's view of God and time likewise enforced his view that God, as God, is wholly unknowable to man. For God is "far from man," beyond "historical reality."[35] God has no developing, unfolding history. There is no middle-ground between God and man on account of their differing relation to time:

> Incomprehensible and meaningless is all confusing of time and eternity… unintelligible and meaningless is all other-worldliness, if other-worldliness is thought of merely as improved worldliness, all improper notions of immanence, every non-radical idea of transcendence, every kind of relative relation between God and man, every divinity which presents itself as being or having or doing what men are or have or do, every human figure which calls itself in any way divine. When all this middle-realm between God and man is clearly recognized, it must be discarded.[36]

35 See Barth, *Dogmatics*, V1.2, 2.16.1 (219).

36 Barth, *Romans*, 108.

On account of God's totally unique relation to time, any and every supposed point of contact between God-in-himself and man must be rejected. Even in Jesus, who is both God and man, man cannot see God-in-himself, properly speaking. Even in Jesus, God-in-himself is concealed from our sight.

Barth defines eternity as a state which encompasses all time simultaneously. Beginning and end are always present to God; he experiences all moments as present. He has no past and no future that was not always present in his static *eternal now*. Barth is justified in appealing to Augustine as a defender of this view. God's sense of time is wholly unique to himself. Likewise, with space, God's space is wholly unique to himself and different from our created space.[37]

Barth acknowledges that the Bible does not portray God as either time-less or as occupying all time all at once. Nor does the Bible define "eternal" as either of these. According to Barth, "The biblical writers do not hesitate to speak of God's years and days, or to describe these as eternal."[38] Barth—like Augustine and Aquinas—concedes that words like "everlasting" in biblical usage refer only to a never-ending duration of time. Of course, they believed the Bible should not be interpreted literally in this regard.

To this point, we find little difference between the views of Barth and Aquinas. Both belong clearly to the same tradition. Barth is incredibly consistent in his defense of simplicity and time-lessness. As such, Barth certainly deserves his place in this survey of classical theists. Clearly, we find a great deal of continuity with the past.

Yet Barth also pushes these ancient doctrines, in some instances, in new and novel directions that represent a departure from the past. Barth famously denies the possibility of natural theology. His reasoning is quite consistent. Since God, as God, is not known to man *at all*, it follows that God is not known to man through the natural world. It

37 See Barth, *Dogmatics*, V2.1, 6.31.1 (p. 487), see V2.1, 6.31.3 (608).

38 Barth, *Dogmatics*, V2.1, 6.31.3 (610).

is, according to Barth, the error of false religion to imagine that God can be inferred from nature.[39] According to Barth, "a 'natural' theology—is quite impossible within the church, and indeed, in such a way that it cannot even be discussed in principle."[40]

In other words, a general revelation of God to all men is a strict impossibility, according to Barth. For if God-in-himself is seen by man in nature, it follows that God-in-himself is not only *knowable* but actually *known* by man by way of inference from creation. Yet that supposes that God and man, grace and nature, are correlated in such a way that God can be inferred from his creation. This would imply that man can know God directly and at least partially univocally, which would seemingly suggest that God and man occupy the same (or at least, very similar) mode of being. Natural theology thus seems to presuppose an epistemological unity between God and man, but Barth insists that "between God and man there is no such unity."[41]

As far as I can see, Barth's reasoning is sound on his own assumptions. If there exists an epistemological divide between God and man on account of each occupying an antithetical mode of being, it follows that man cannot reason his way across this divide. God cannot, in that case, be revealed in nature. Barth is thus consistent in concluding (much like Dionysius) that God remains altogether "unrevealed" to those without God's special revelation.[42]

Of course, Barth can hardly fail to recognize that the biblical authors commonly speak about seeing God in nature. Passages such as Psalm 19 readily come to mind:

> The heavens tell of the glory of God;
> And their expanse declares the work of His hands.

---

39 See *Dogmatics*, V1.2, 2.17.2 (301).

40 Barth, *Dogmatics*, V2.1, 5.26.1 (85).

41 Barth, *Dogmatics*, V2.1, 5.27.1 (189).

42 See Barth, *Dogmatics*, V2.1, 5.26.1 (109).

> Day to day pours forth speech,
> And night to night reveals knowledge.
> There is no speech, nor are there words;
> Their voice is not heard.
> Their line has gone out into all the earth,
> And their words to the end of the world. (Psalm 19:1-4a)

Barth's answer is that there is indeed a proper place for a theology of nature, yet he insists that such a theology is always subsequent to the experience of grace. Barth is quick to emphasize that the psalmists were already men of faith who had encountered God's Word of special revelation, and were thus free to read God's special, revealed goodness back into nature.

Ignoring for the moment Barth's questionable biblical exegesis on this point, he is certainly more consistent than Aquinas. Aquinas held that God occupies a contrary mode of being from man, but that man could nevertheless infer God's existence, at least, from nature. Barth has forever solidified the point that these two notions of Aquinas stand in contradiction to one another. If God is completely "other" than nature in the sense of being epistemologically antithetical to nature, it certainly follows that we cannot reason our way from nature to God. To put it succinctly, God's simple, time-less existence could never be inferred from the manifold, temporal realm of nature.

That's not to say that I agree with Barth's view, of course. Where Aquinas attempted to balance, to some extent at least, the demands of the Bible against the demands of an implicit Neoplatonic metaphysic, Barth, to a much greater extent, subordinates the Bible to the Platonic Divorce. We will continue to see that it is precisely his consistency to the Neoplatonic principles of classical theism that perpetually drew him into conflict with Protestant orthodoxy and, in my view, with the Bible itself.

That the Apostle Paul *explicitly* said that God is evident to all men through nature seems a natural objection to Barth's view that

God cannot be inferred from nature. Thanks in large part to Barth, chapter one of the book of Romans was almost certainly the most widely discussed biblical passage in the twentieth century. There the Apostle wrote:

> For the wrath of God is revealed from heaven against all ungodliness and unrighteousness of people who suppress the truth in unrighteousness, because that which is known about God is evident within them; for God made it evident to them. For since the creation of the world His invisible attributes, that is, His eternal power and divine nature, have been clearly perceived, being understood by what has been made, so that they are without excuse. For even though they knew God, they did not honor Him as God or give thanks, but they became futile in their reasonings, and their senseless hearts were darkened. Claiming to be wise, they became fools, and they exchanged the glory of the incorruptible God for an image in the form of corruptible mankind, of birds, four-footed animals, and crawling creatures. (Romans 1:18-23)

Paul's view was that God is "clearly perceived" via "what has been made." Though all men derive a natural knowledge of God from nature, they nevertheless "suppress" this knowledge on account of moral unrighteousness. It is on account of this natural knowledge of God that all men will be held accountable to God. This is the plain, unforced interpretation of the passage.

What is Barth's view of the passage? Fortunately for us, we need not speculate for Barth wrote a commentary on the book of Romans. Barth argues that what is "clearly revealed" from heaven is that God is totally distinct from us, and thus totally unknowable. Plato is commended as an example of this perception.[43] The great error of man, according

43 See Barth, *Romans*, 46.

to Barth, lies in thinking that God can be known to man, and against such a notion the wrath of God is revealed. Thinking that we can know anything about the unknowable or incorruptible God is turning God into an image of creation (four-footed beasts and the like). On account of this arrogant sin of presuming to know something about God, God gives us over to *known and knowable* gods, which are, of course, merely the false gods of human imagination, since God himself is strictly unknowable.

This is clearly a fanciful interpretation of the passage. Barth has obviously forced the passage to fit a preconceived philosophical mold; Barth has made Paul into Plotinus. On Barth's reading, there would be no justification for God to be wrathful regarding the suppression of truth by sinful man, for man can hardly be expected to know what he *cannot possibly* know. There would be no grounds for God to condemn that man whom the gospel had not yet reached. This is one of many tendencies in Barth which seems to suggest a universal salvation for all men. Barth is, by all accounts, consistent in his refusal to deny a universal salvation for all. Of course, if all men are eventually saved, there does not seem to be any particularly pressing reason to be a Christian. Pantheism, Mohammedism, or atheism will do just as well in that case.

Alongside Barth's rejection of natural theology comes his rejection of Christian apologetics. Barth believes the practice of apologetics should be abandoned as both useless and impossible. Barth's reasoning is again straightforward, logical, and consistent. If a Christian is to persuade the atheist, for example, that God exists, he must argue from premises that both parties formally accept. Beginning with certain well-established human premises, the Christian must gradually work his way to a knowledge of God. He can argue, for example, that nature suggests design and that design, in turn, suggests some great intelligence. He may further argue that this particular type of creation supposes a Creator of a certain sort and that the God of the Bible fits the bill.

Yet in order for this type of argument to yield legitimate results, God must, once again, be a valid inference from nature. *Apologetics, no less than natural theology, must presuppose some common epistemological ground between God and man.* Without the assumption of epistemological similarity and likeness between God and man, the apologetic enterprise becomes a non-starter.

Barth strenuously rejects the premise that there is any epistemic commonality between God and man and so is consistent in denying the possibility of reasoning one's way to God via Christian apologetics. In a passage very reminiscent of Plotinus, Barth insists that God cannot be inferred from nature:

> God does not belong to the world. Therefore He does not belong to the series of objects for which we have categories and words by means of which we draw the attention of others to them, and bring them into relation with them. Of God it is impossible to speak, because he is neither a natural nor a spiritual object. If we speak of Him, we are no longer speaking of Him. In this matter we cannot do what we want to do and we cannot attain what we should like to attain. This is the iron law under which all Church proclamation without exception stands. That what happens here happens in frailty is far too weak an expression for the real situation. This is not frailty. It is death. This is not difficulty. It is sheer impossibility. What happens here is not something imperfect. Measured by the standard of what is intended, it is simply nothing.[44]

Barth's rejection of the apologetic endeavor is entirely consistent with his rejection of a natural knowledge of God. God cannot be inferred from nature, for God—as simple and time-less—is wholly

44 Barth, *Dogmatics*, V1.2, 4.22.1 (750).

unlike nature. Man cannot reason his way to God, for God and man cannot speak the same language or think in the same terms.

It is on this same basis that Barth also rejects the doctrine of the verbal Inspiration of Scripture. His reasoning is, once again, straightforward. Since God's thoughts are simple, and our thoughts are not simple, since God's thoughts are time-less and our thoughts are temporal, God and man have no comparable thoughts. It follows, in such a situation, that God cannot communicate directly with man. Inspiration, according to Barth, supposes that "a real human word is the real Word of God"[45] but God and man cannot speak the same language because they have no point of epistemological contact. God and man are antithetical; they have absolutely nothing in common epistemologically.

Here we may well recall Augustine's difficulty in imagining God the Father speaking the words "This is my beloved Son," one syllable at a time, into the temporal world. Barth has pushed the same difficulty a step further and his conclusion is more consistent than that of Augustine, who suggested that angelic intermediaries relayed the message between God's time-lessness and our time.

For Barth, the epistemological separation between God and man is total. The divorce is comprehensive. Man cannot understand divine speech for divine speech would necessarily have to be in time-less and simple terms. Barth argues that where humans speak *human*, only God speaks divine. Accordingly, "We cannot force them [i.e., prophets and apostles] to do and speak the Word of God in their human words."[46] God cannot speak human, nor can humans speak divine, for God occupies an antithetical mode of being. Man is trapped in one cave; God is trapped in another.

There is no divine truth in our human doctrine, according to Barth. All human doctrine is merely human doctrine. "Humanly speaking,"

---

45 Barth, *Dogmatics*, V1.2, 2.19.2 (518).

46 Barth, *Dogmatics*, V1.2, 2.19.2 (533).

said Barth, "is the only way we can speak."[47] Smugly and rhetorically, Barth asks, "Can a doctrinal proposition as such really be regarded as God's Word?"[48] Here again, Barth is faithful to his own assumptions. The doctrine of a verbal, plenary Inspiration supposes the *identity* of divine speech with human speech inasmuch as the words of the Bible are imagined to be concurrently written by both the Holy Spirit and the human author. The Doctrine of Inspiration says, in short, that humans penned *divine* words. Yet this seems to suppose that God and man share some common epistemological core such that there can be a free translation of divine things into human speech and vice versa. The doctrine of Inspiration requires that a divine word can be a human word and a human word can be a divine word. The Doctrine of Inspiration thus seems to assume univocal communication between God and man, but Barth will not allow this.

So God, as God, according to Barth, is found neither in nature nor in Scripture. Having closed these avenues to us, Barth points us to yet another source of knowledge. For Barth, God's clearest and best revelation is to be sought only in the person of Jesus Christ. He is the true revelation of God to man, being himself both God and man. Jesus is the point where the known and unknown meet. "In this name two worlds meet and go apart, two planes intersect, the one known and the other unknown.... The name Jesus defines an historical occurrence and marks the point where the unknown world cuts the known world."[49]

It might be tempting, at this juncture, to jump to the conclusion that Barth believed Jesus bridged the epistemological chasm that divides God and man. That is not his view; Barth will not betray his own position at this point. Even Jesus cannot be viewed as establishing

47 Barth, *Dogmatics*, V1.1, 1.7.2 (282).

48 Barth, *Dogmatics*, V1.1, 1.7.1 (271). Here again, Barth seems to conflate two things, as though God himself were a piece of propositional knowledge. This seems, once again, a straw man.

49 Barth, *Romans*, 29.

an epistemological middle-ground between God-in-himself and man, for "there exists no third and intermediate thing between the Unknown God [!] and the altogether too well-known world."[50]

Who or what then is Jesus? Jesus is God's "self-objectification."[51] Though God-in-himself cannot reveal himself to us, he reveals himself to us as a human object, in the human mode. Jesus is "God's entry into the sphere of the creature and therefore into the sphere and the limits of our comprehensibility."[52] Though God-in-himself cannot reveal himself to us as he really is, he comes to us concealed in a "secular" medium. "If God did not speak to us in secular form, He would not speak to us at all."[53] Apart from this gracious act of God humanizing and secularizing himself, we could not know God. "The veil is thick. We do not have the Word of God otherwise than in the mystery of its secularity."[54] In a particularly lucid passage, Barth says that Jesus can be thought of as God's humanized *alter ego*:

> No matter who or what else the self-revealing God may be, it is beyond dispute that in His revelation according to the biblical witness He takes form, and this taking form is His self-unveiling. It is not impossible nor is it too petty a thing for Him to be His own *alter ego* in His revelation, His *alter ego* to the extent that His self-unveiling, His taking form, obviously cannot be taken for granted but is an event, and an event that cannot be explained by or derived from either the will or act of man or the course of the world at large; to the extent that He Himself must take a step towards this event; to the extent that this step obviously means something new in God, a self-distinction of God from Himself,

50 Barth, *Romans*, 323.

51 Barth, *Dogmatics*, V1.1, 1.4.1 (92).

52 Barth, *Dogmatics*, V1.1, 2.9.4 (374).

53 Barth, *Dogmatics*, V1.1, 1.5.4 (168).

54 Barth, *Dogmatics*, V1.1, 1.5.4 (165).

> a being of God in a mode of being that is different from though not subordinate to His first and hidden mode of being as God, in a mode of being, of course, in which He can also exist for us. The God who reveals Himself here can reveal Himself. The very fact of revelation tells us that it is proper to Him to distinguish Himself from Himself, i.e. to be God in Himself and in concealment, and yet at the same time to be God a second time in a very different way, namely in manifestation, i.e., in the form of something He himself is not.[55]

God-in-himself is unknown to us. God-as-revealed in Jesus is God's self-objectification and self-humanization. Paradoxically, the God of Scripture is found by us "in the form of something He is not." In the revelation that is the person of Christ, God presents himself as altogether unlike himself:

> Biblical revelation consists in the freedom of God to differentiate Himself from Himself, to become unlike Himself and yet to remain the same, to be indeed the one God like Himself and to exist as the one sole God in the fact that in this way that is so inconceivably profound He differentiates Himself from Himself.[56]

The only way we can see God is if God is entirely humanized.[57] Barth understands Christ's *kenosis* or self-emptying (see e.g., Philippians 2:7) as his complete hiddenness *as God*. Thus, Jesus belongs clearly to the human mode of being for Barth. That is not to say that Barth denies Jesus' divinity, for he quite clearly affirms it. It is, however, to say that we cannot rationally or sensibly see that which is *properly divine*

55 Barth, *Dogmatics*, V1.1, 2.8.2 (316). Emphasis in original.

56 Barth, *Dogmatics*, V1.1, 2.8.2 (320).

57 See Barth, *Romans*, 279.

in Christ: "Thus God's becoming man means undoubtedly in the first instance that His divinity becomes latent."[58] Strictly speaking, we cannot see the *divine* in Christ, we can only see the human. We saw precisely the same teaching in Dionysius.

Barth offers several reasons for this view. For one, Jesus walked about in time, but God is time-less. Therefore, according to Barth, we know that what we see in Jesus is not properly divine. "In the revelation in Jesus" we can see that "God can become unlike Himself in such a way that He is not tied to His secret eternity and eternal secrecy but can and will and does in fact take temporal form as well."[59]

Barth finds additional support for this view in the biblical affirmation that Jesus was discovered "in the likeness of sinful flesh" (Romans 8:3), which he takes to mean the total concealment of God-in-himself in a fallen, human form. "There is then no mission of the Son except—in the likeness of sin-controlled flesh, except in the form of a servant, except in His impenetrable incognito."[60] Just as the Christian sacraments are signs that direct us to some other, secret, hidden reality, so too Jesus is a sign and an image that perfectly conceals God-in-himself even as he reveals God-as-revealed. "Under this image, under this incognito, the Son of God came into the world."[61]

Having clothed himself in humanity in the person of Christ, God is unveiled to us, and yet God-in-himself remains entirely concealed and hidden from our view. Barth strenuously emphasizes the paradox of this disclosure:

> He unveils himself as the One He is by veiling Himself in a form which He Himself is not. He uses this form distinct from Himself, He uses its work and sign, in order to be

58 Barth, *Dogmatics*, V1.2, 2.13.2 (38).

59 Barth, *Dogmatics*, V1.1, 2.8.2 (320).

60 Barth, *Romans*, 279.

61 Barth, *Romans*, 323.

> objective in, with and under this form, and therefore to give Himself to us to be known. Revelation means the giving of signs. We can say quite simply that revelation means sacrament, i.e., the self-witness of God, the representation of His truth, and therefore of the truth in which He knows Himself, in the form of creaturely objectivity and therefore in a form which is adapted to our creaturely knowledge.[62]

Barth's position is really quite similar to that of Dionysius. God is known only through his effects. He reveals himself to us only in creaturely guise. God-in-himself is entirely unknown to us, whereas God-as-revealed is known to us, but, unfortunately, completely unlike his true self, which is simple and time-less. Paradoxically, God is concealed in Jesus even as he is revealed in Jesus. "In Jesus God is known to be the unknown God."[63] As God incognito, Jesus hides God from us just as surely as he reveals God to us in human guise. "In Jesus, God becomes veritably a secret: He is made known as the Unknown, speaking in eternal silence."[64] Jesus thus presents us with "The Gospel of the Unknown God."[65]

Like Dionysius, Barth concedes that the human knowledge of God is really only a self-reflection of man: "Our supposed idea of God, the object of our most intimate feeling, will always be the idea of the world and in the last resort of man."[66] The divide between God and man is comprehensive and exhaustive. Our idea of God is only a "supposed idea." All of our theological God-talk is really just anthropological man-talk.

Barth seems to offer something of a critique of his own view when he says that we must always fight against our discontent regarding the

---

62 Barth, *Dogmatics*, V2.1, 5.25.2 (52).

63 Barth, *Romans*, 114.

64 Barth, *Romans*, 98.

65 Barth, *Romans*, 377.

66 Barth, *Dogmatics*, V2.1, 5.27.2 (228).

fact that we can never get behind the veil of our fully human revelation to see anything of the properly divine. Man is forever doomed to harbor the suspicion that the real God is quite unlike the God disclosed to us in Scripture. For God's revelation is:

> grounded more in the nature of the world, and in our own nature, than in the nature of God Himself. This [divine] nature itself, as the proper being of God, has to be regarded as standing inscrutably beyond and above this economy. That God is mighty, holy, just, merciful, omnipresent, is affirmed more in relation to an analogical world in which He exists for us than in relation to His being in itself as it is in reality. In this case, faith in Him can never completely free itself from *ultimate suspicion* in face of a Lord whom it pleases to yield Himself to us in this or that form in a kind of sport, without disclosing Himself in reality, without giving us any pledge that in Himself He is not perhaps quite other, and so radically different from the forms of glory in the game played with us that it is not worth while perhaps to take part in this game or this economy.[67]

Man can never be content knowing God is fully unknown to him. Man is forever doomed to harbor the suspicion—indeed, the conviction!—that the God he discovers in Scripture is nothing like the real God. Barth admits dissatisfaction with his own position, and for good reason. Notice that by "analogical," Barth does not mean that we have a little bit of knowledge of God-in-himself. Rather, he means that the biblical witness contains only a self-reflection of man. Upon inspection, our "analogical knowledge of God" turns out really to be only a knowledge of man. Properly speaking, it is not a knowledge of *God* at all. Of God, as God, we have no knowledge whatsoever.

---

67 Barth, *Dogmatics*, V2.1, 6.29.1 (324).

If I may again interject as the simpleton that I am, it seems to me very misleading to say that we have an "analogical knowledge of God," when we really only mean that we have a knowledge of God that is wholly human and thus wholly unlike God. In such a case, we're merely covering over our comprehensive ignorance with a fancy, pretentious term. It seems to me something like the decorative housing that conceals the unsightly toilet plunger in my bathroom.

Barth's view is remarkably consistent with the premise that God occupies a different mode of being than man. God, as God, cannot be known in nature, nor in Scripture, nor even in Jesus Christ. God, as God, is unspeakable and unknowable. On the Platonic and Neoplatonic premise of an epistemological divorce between God and man, such conclusions are inevitable.

Where Augustine and Aquinas tried—unsuccessfully—to balance the Bible against the philosophical principles of Platonism, it seems clear that Barth, to a much greater extent, subordinates the Bible to the Platonic Divorce. Barth repeatedly demonstrates that he is willing to jettison biblical doctrines in order to be a consistent classical theist.

Though my disagreements with Barth span the entire extent of Christian Theology, I cannot deny that the sheer scope of Barth's massive *Church Dogmatics* as well as the impressive intensity of his logical rigor and astonishing degree of internal consistency will make him a model of systematic theology for some time to come. Much could also be said about the fertile field that resulted from the rebuttal to Barth. The seedling field of presuppositional apologetics, for example, was a direct response to Barth, and was, as such, unthinkable apart from Barth. Many thinkers seemed to capitulate to Barth as they abandoned the old "evidential" attempt to reason their way to God. They proposed attacking the enemy's view rather than dwelling much on the rational merits of their own. Many seemed to concede the point to Barth that faith requires an irrational leap into the arms of the UNKNOWN.

The present work also undoubtedly owes a debt to Barth. Barth pushed an implicit Platonism to its logical conclusion and demonstrated that something is surely amiss. To the extent that Barth admonished us to stop looking for *God* in theology, he seems a fitting end to our historical survey of classical theism. Clearly, Barth brings us to a crossroad.

11

Conclusion

WE have undoubtedly seen a consistent pattern: a simple God cannot be known to those of us who are not simple. A time-less God cannot be known to the temporal. An epistemological chasm is opened between God and man on account of these teachings. An awkward distinction is made between God-in-himself and God-as-revealed.

Classical theists imagine that the temporal and manifold God portrayed in Scripture is suitable for children and simpletons, while the mature are to move beyond this superficial presentation so as to understand that the real God is simple, time-less, and, therefore, unknowable. The great irony, in such a case, is that God is discovered neither in Scripture *nor beyond it*. For the God discovered beyond Scripture is simultaneously discovered to be unknowable. In that very moment in which we deny that we have a *proper* knowledge of God in Scripture, we simultaneously deny that we have any knowledge of God at all. We presume the folly of knowing the unknown; we revel in a shallow mysticism.

It seems to me (simpleton that I am) that the apathy that abounds on every side in our day—indeed, the agnosticism and atheism—is little more than the consistent outworking of classical theism which complained for two thousand years that God is, in the last analysis, unknown and unrevealed to us. We proclaimed him UNKNOWN and, surely enough, he became unknown to us; we received precisely what we asked for; we attained the ignorance we worshipped. We scorned his revelation by presuming to look past it, but what we found past it was neither reasonable nor satisfying.

Should health, strength, and interest continue, I hope to offer a second volume in the series in which I will make a more direct and open refutation of classical theism. The present volume seemed a necessary first step unto that ultimate (or perhaps penultimate) end. I hope to further explore the modern revolt against classical theism, to demonstrate that many of the biblical passages used to defend it are unjustly wrenched out of context, and to exposit relational theism as a more intuitive, biblical alternative.

For the present, I think it fitting to take my seat among the children.

Bibliography

Adams, Marilyn McCord. *William Ockham*. Notre Dame, Indiana: University of Notre Dame Press. 1987.

Alston, William, editor. *Realism & Antirealism*. Ithaca and London: Cornell University Press. 2002.

Aristotle. *Great Books of the Western World, Volume 7*. Chicago, Illinois: Encyclopaedia Britannica. 1993.

Augustine. *Great Books of the Western World, Volume 16*. Chicago, Illinois: Encyclopaedia Britannica. 1993.

Augustine. *Eighty-Three Different Questions*. Washington D.C.: The Catholic University of America Press. 1982.

Augustine. *The Trinity*. Hyde Park, New York: New City Press. 1991.

Aquinas. *Great Books of the Western World, Volume 17*. Chicago, Illinois: Encyclopaedia Britannica. 1993.

Baines, Ronald S., editor. *Confessing the Impassible God: The Biblical, Classical, & Confessional Doctrine of Divine Impassibility*. Palmdale, California: RBAP. 2015.

Bardon, Adrian. *A Brief History of the Philosophy of Time*. Oxford: Oxford University Press. 2013.

Barth, Karl. *Church Dogmatics. I.1: The Doctrine of the Word of God.* Edinburgh: T&T Clark. 1975.

Barth, Karl. *Church Dogmatics. I.2: The Doctrine of the Word of God.* Edinburgh: T&T Clark. 1975.

Barth, Karl. *Church Dogmatics. II.1.: The Doctrine of God.* Edinburgh: T&T Clark. 1975.

Brock, Stuart and Edwin Mares. *Realism and Anti-Realism.* Montreal and Kingston: McGill-Queen's University Press. 2007.

Castelo, Daniel. *The Apathetic God: Exploring the Contemporary Relevance of Divine Impassibility.* Eugene, Oregon: Wipf and Stock Publishers. 2009.

Clement of Alexandria. Schaff, Philip, ed. *The Complete Anti-Nicene & Nicene & Post-Nicene Church Fathers Collection.* London, England: Catholic Way Publishing. Kindle Edition. 2014.

Coogan, Michael D., ed. *The New Oxford Annotated Apocrypha.* New York, New York: Oxford University Press. 2001.

Copleston, Frederick. *A History of Philosophy*, Volumes 1-6. New York, New York: Doubleday. 1993.

Dionysius the Areopagite, *The Works of.* Unknown: Aeterna Press. 2014.

Dolezal, James E. *God without Parts: Divine Simplicity and the Metaphysics of God's Absoluteness.* Eugene, Oregon: Pickwick Publications. 2011.

Duby, Steven J. *Divine Simplicity: A Dogmatic Account.* London, England: Bloomsbury. 2016.

Edwards, Jonathan. *Works, Volume 21: Writing on the Trinity, Grace, and Faith.* Binghamton, New York: Yale University Press. 2003.

Fitzgerald, Allan, editor. *Augustine Through the Ages.* Grand Rapids, Michigan: William B. Eerdmans Publishing. 1999.

Hinlicky, Paul R. *Divine Simplicity: Christ the Crisis of Metaphysics.* Grand Rapids, Michigan: Baker Academic. 2016.

Hodge, Charles. *Systematic Theology.* Grand Rapids, Michigan: William B. Eerdmans Publishing. Unspecified.

Holford-Stevens, Leofranc. *The History of Time.* Oxford: Oxford University Press. 2005.

Inge, William Ralph. *The Philosophy of Plotinus: The Gifford Lectures at St. Andrews 1917-1918.* Westport, Connecticut: Greenwood Press. 1968.

Kenny, Anthony. *A New History of Western Philosophy.* New York: Oxford University Press. 2010.

Kenny, Anthony. *The God of the Philosophers.* Oxford: Oxford University Press. 1986.

Kuhn, Thomas S. *The Structure of Scientific Revolutions.* Chicago, Illinois: University of Chicago Press. 1996.

Le Poideven, Robin & Murray MacBeath, editors. *The Philosophy of Time.* Oxford: Oxford University Press. 2009.

Luscombe, David. *Medieval Thought.* Oxford: Oxford University Press. 1997.

Matz, Robert J. *Divine Impassibility: Four Views of God's Emotions and Suffering.* Downers Grove, Illinois: IVP Academic. 2019.

Minich, Joseph & Onsi A. Kamel, Editors. *The Lord is One: Reclaiming Divine Simplicity.* Landrum, South Carolina: Davenant Press. 2019.

Mozley, J.K. *The Impassibility of God: A Survey of Christian Thought.* London, England: Cambridge University Press. 1927.

Mullins, R.T. *Simply Impossible: A Case Against Divine Simplicity.* Journal of Reformed Theology 7 (2013) 181-203.

Ney, Alyssa. *Metaphysics: An Introduction.* London and New York: Routledge. 2014.

Ockham: *Philosophical Writings.* Indianapolis, Indiana: Hackett Publishing Company. 1990.

Pelikan, Jaroslav. *The Christian Tradition: Volume 1: The Emergence of the Catholic Tradition.* Chicago: University of Chicago Press. 1971.

Plato. *Great Books of the Western World, Volume 6.* Chicago, Illinois: Encyclopaedia Britannica. 1993.

Plotinus. *Great Books of the Western World, Volume 11.* Chicago, Illinois: Encyclopedia Britannica. 1993.

Richards, Jay Wesley. *The Untamed God: A Philosophical Exploration of Divine Perfections, Immutability, and Simplicity.* Downers Grove, Illinois: InterVarsity Press. 2003.

Russell, Bertrand. *A History of Western Philosophy.* New York: Simon & Schuster. 1972.

Spade, Paul Vincent, editor. *Five Texts on the Mediaeval Problem of Universals: Porphyry, Boethius, Abelard, Duns Scotus, Ockham. Indianapolis, Indiana: Hackett Publishing Company.* 1994.

Turetzky, Philip. *Time.* New York: Routledge. 1998.

Warfield, Benjamin Breckinridge. *The Person and Work of Christ.* Philadelphia, Pennsylvania: P&R. 1970.

Wolterstorff, Nicholas. *Inquiring About God: Selected Essays, Volume I.* New York: Cambridge University Press. 2014.

www.ingramcontent.com/pod-product-compliance
Lightning Source LLC
LaVergne TN
LVHW020709110826
845149LV00012B/2181

* 9 7 8 0 9 9 0 8 0 0 8 6 6 *